SOMETHING TO SMILE ABOUT

A Journey into the True Heart of Jamaica

by Isaac Hye

Taderon Press
London

This publication was made possible with a generous donation from Clara and George Vosbigian.

Originally published by Jamedia Media Productions Ltd., P.O. Box 727, Kingston 6, JA *jamediapro@hotmail.com*, July 2022. Reprinted with permission by the Taderon Press (London).

ISBN: 978-1-909382-78-8

For comments or more information please contact:
TaderonPress@gmail.com

CONTENTS

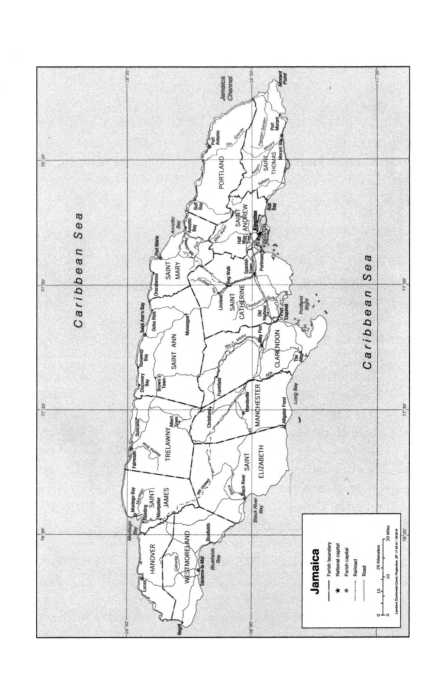

Preface to New Edition

As you will read herein, Jamaica was initially a dream for me, a real place with attached appendages that were the product of my own imagination. As such, when the dream became a reality and I got to visit this wonderful and mysterious country, I wanted to document my journey in detail. After all how many of us get to truly realise our dreams?

I wrote thousands of words every night that I was there (power cuts pending), and then on my return tucked it away in the box marked *aim to get round to it, but probably won't.*

When Covid hit I was absent-mindedly clearing my computer and found the text that you now have in your hands. It bought back vivid and joyous memories so I shared sections of it with my friend, the artist Alfie Benge, and it was she who was responsible for persuading me to make it public. I began to post chapters online and out of the blue the wonderful Barbara Makeda Blake-Hannah came across them and messaged me saying that she looked forward to it being published. I told her that I hadn't thought of such a scenario nor would I know how to go about it, to which she responded with the offer of help. Barbara is a well known figure in both Britain and Jamaica, having been the first Black woman on British television, an M.P. back in Jamaica as well as being a celebrated author read worldwide. Needless to say, I felt Jah blessed to have her on my side! It was Barbara who was responsible for the first edition being published in Jamaica which was then picked up by Ara Sarafian who enjoyed my take on Jamaica and is responsible for the copy you are now reading in your hands.

To all three of these lovely people I am very grateful.

Others I would like to thank for their encouragement on this side of the Atlantic are Jamie Sharrock and Emyr Glyn

Williams who have consistently provided me with positive vibes, the latter introducing me to the wonderful reggae Cymraeg world of Geraint Jarman; Dionne Bennett for her Britsh/Jamaican perspective and support, Graham Ennis of When Skies Are Grey for allowing my ganja addled ramblings to take shape in his august journal and Ryan Jones for the same. Thanks is also proffered to my father who had a thing for Jamaican athlete Grace Jackson (!) and who encouraged my love for West Indian cricket, my family for putting up with what latterly became a passion project and not judging the content therein when there was much to be judged; and to the many other friends who have unwittingly encouraged me with kind comments. Thanks also to the magnificent organisers of Sumfest who enabled me to pretend to be a journalist, to Howard Marks (much missed) for some wonderful chats about Jamaica, and of course thanks also to my dealers everywhere.

On the Jamaican side I would like to thank every single person who is mentioned in the book for better or worse, be they Jamaican reggae artistes; locals from the length and breadth of the island that I encountered, or gargantuan fellow plane passengers, because they all made the whole experience truly unforgettable.

Most importantly I would like to thank my extended Jamaican family who gave me a love, warmth and welcome that I can't imagine ever being matched. They are quite simply, beautiful people. The adoration I have for them is eternal. Sadly, Pops is no longer with us, and given that he was the most splendid human being I have ever met, it is to him that this book is dedicated.

Ites,

Isaac Hye.

6 January, 2024

Introduction by
Barbara Makeda Blake Hannah

Isaac Hye books a trip from Britain to Jamaica for Reggae Sumfest and decides to stay with a Jamaican family, rather than at an all-inclusive hotel. His one-month stay with a family in Pleasantown, St. Ann is the topic of this hilarious book, a story told with British deadpan humour and a surprising knowledge of culture and history that reveals a tender love of Jamaica and polishes the rough edges of our tropic island into a very shining and unusual *Journey Into The True Heart Of Jamaica*.

Meet Ras Kelvin, DeeDee, Poochie, their friends Radar, the driver ("always trying to break the land speed record") and Buzzy, ("both of whom seem like real gentlemen...especially to the ladiessssssss") and several children Mo, Snoop, TJ, Kaddy and Jay, DeeDee's other children. There is Pops, whose welcome gift is a large bag of ganja, and Momma – who is the house's real authority. "When Momma says 'Jump', these kids try to break the Olympic record."

We travel with Hye and the family on several adventurous and hair-raising journeys speeding on Jamaica's many 'bad' roads, for shopping trips to Ocho Rios, visits to family in St. Elizabeth and the doctor in Kingston. There are stops at historic Jamaican birthplaces and moments of National Heroes Alexander Bustamante, Marcus Garvey and Paul Bogle, as well as a chapter that describes a memorable visit to Bob Marley's Nine Miles birthplace.

Most of all, he meets simple, everyday Jamaicans. "Jamaica, and more importantly its people, were everything I could have

Disappearing into Fern Gully

possibly hoped for." He takes the ball at a beachside football game, attends a hilarious cricket match at a country village, enjoys Poochie's birthday party on Emancipation Day and the drums of a Rastafari celebration of the Emperor's July 23rd Birthday.

All, before finally spending three sleepless nights taking in the music, crowds and amazing sights, sounds and atmosphere of Reggae Sumfest, which he declares is not only the Greatest Reggae Show on Earth, but "the greatest show on Earth, period!"

Accredited as a journalist, Hye takes the reader backstage and into the cordoned, exclusive media room, giving a description of the reggae artists and people who take up residence there for three nights jostling for couch space and interviews with the world's greatest reggae artists. He reports on his interviews with them and gives his opinion of their performances, from the scandal-filled Dancehall Night, to the two nights of roots and regular Reggae. It's a view rarely shared of the engine of Jamaica's most popular music show. ("Dancehall Night was quite simply the most fantastic spectacle I have ever witnessed.")

Hye's farewell from the family who have become part of his life is a summary of all that makes Jamaica such a wonderful country and its people so special. ("Jamaicans smiling and laughing through their tough lives.") The reader shares his tears because his words describe how great our island is when seen through the eyes of others who understand how far Jamaica has come from a country of enslaved Africans without land or wealth, to a beautiful nation that could be a true Paradise, if only...

Something To Smile About is a step across the racial and cultural bridge that shows how White people should relate to and live with Black people and it is an unusual story, told with endless laugh-out-loud moments. It is definitely worth reading by all Jamaicans and visitors who love and are proud of Jamaican culture.

—Barbara Makeda Blake-Hannah, O.S.E., O.D.
Cultural Liaison, Ministry of Culture, author of *Growing Out : Black Hair and Black Pride in the* Swinging 60s, Kingston, Jamaica

SOMETHING TO SMILE ABOUT

A Journey into the
True Heart of Jamaica

Chapter One

Flight And Arrival

Kerchuuuuunk!

The searing sound of concrete on metal was me mounting the kerb outside the south terminal of Gatwick Airport. I was sober because I had not yet started my prerequisite to flying-binge, the intended enormity of which would have the Government issuing new health warnings and my fellow passengers wishing they had caught a later flight. No, the reason for my 'minor' misjudgement was due to my left contact lens mysteriously splitting as I was halfway down the M11, and I had therefore initially been using 'one eye shut Cyclopic vision' with which to drive until it became too unbearable, so I had ditched the other lens and was now driving 'blind'. The damage to the car was minimal, however the psychological damage was wrought in one who, on reaching the airport entrance, was further traumatised by the realisation he would not be sparking up a smoke again for at least twelve hours.

This was not the most auspicious start to my adventure. Jamaica: the destination I had dreamt about since being a child, the place where I would finally absorb the aura of mystery and myth and feel the pulsating beats of the annual Sumfest reggae festival which was the main reason for my trip. I was hauled out of my dreamlike state by a nagging voice in my head:

"You must get there first": which means flying.

I have been on several flights over the years, but the fear does not decrease. Every time I step onto one of those potential coffins in the sky, I have, at least metaphorically, soiled my pants.

I consider myself to be a logical human being, well, logical, but still the concept of a huge hunk of heavy metal with 400 people on board being launched into the air and staying there has never entirely convinced me of its feasibility. I began to drink readily and steadily (just not enough to alarm the airport authorities) in order that I would be passed out for most of the journey. It would also ensure that I would not overly concern the passengers by allowing them the spectacle of belligerence that is a smoker denied his fix, even when it may be his last. I just wanted to get on the plane, get loaded, and get knocked out.

At passport control the usual standoff ensued where they look at my photograph and name, then look at me again, then at my photograph and name, then me again.

"Isaac?"

"Yes, a madness on the part of my father".

"Hye?"

"Yes, a madness on the part of an Armenian ancestor way back".

"So, Isaac Hye?"

"Yes", I sighed. My eyes narrowed as I watched the officer make the inevitable connection and formulate what he considered to be a highly unique joke, yet one I had heard several times before in various situations.

"Don't be getting 'Hye' in Jamaica!" he laughed, as if this was the funniest joke he had ever heard.

"I won't", I lied with a mirrored laugh, because I intended scoring some weed as soon as I exited the airport at the other end.

As I boarded, I was moved to witness the Ark-ian procession that was my fellow passengers. This was a truly international flock of flavour, all heading to their own special and imagined paradise. The one who decided to sit in front of me, however, was an enormous flocker. After an interminable wait for late arrivals, I began to look around the plane but all I could see was the back of a big, fat, football shaped head. Fortunately, the TV screens were on the seat in front. Unfortunately, FAT FOOTBALL HEAD reclined so far back that I had to twist my back and neck just to see the screen. I asked kindly that he might alter the level of his seat. In return I received a volley of "Bumbaclaat!", "Cho!", and an impressive number of teeth sucking. I politely suggested he refrain from talking in such a manner, to which his response was to ask if I was going to "Shut my face for me then?" It then dissolved into a low-level bout of sniping before a steward stepped in and asked if everything was alright. The journey thereafter was like a pair of lovers having had a tiff, trying not to make eye contact, folding of arms etc. 1-0 to nicotine.

I hate travelling with the public. I am a terrible hypochondriac and even though this journey took place pre-Covid, the slightest cough or sneeze could send me dizzy into praying for a handily place surgical mask or at least something to prevent that germ heading towards *me*.

In a similar vein, I despise aeroplane toilets. There is never enough room to move about in, and you feel under constant pressure to perform knowing that there is likely to be a queue outside. This flight contained another obstacle to a normal lavatorial procedure. Every time I went down the aisle to the toilet, I had to squeeze past two be-suited types, with matching bellies and sweaty faces. You guessed it; they were two of Her Majesty's finest returning a son back to his motherland, for what misdemeanour I don't know, but it is a common story for Jamaicans in the UK, and especially so under the current culture-war Government. All I can tell you is that it is not much fun trying to squeeze between two gargantuan guts and four perspiring armpits to answer the call of nature. Richard Branson, you have a lot to answer for. I wonder if when you go round to Branson's on a party night, he finds you the smallest chair in the house; shoehorns you in, straps a belt around you, lowers the seat in front to its maximum, puts an elephantine man on that seat, feeds you with food that tastes like rubber, and then charges you for the 'pleasure'? I knew that by the end of this flight I would be walking like a giraffe with rickets, would smell awful and have an appalling taste in my mouth, which I suppose, for my generation and younger, constitutes the end of any great night out. And then, as if on cue, the drinks trolley arrived to save my flight.

God Bless Richard Branson!

I opted for a Vodka and Coke...well the choice is limited, and then commanded the rest of my neighbouring, teetotal, God-fearing row to order a spirit along with their soft drink which they should then pass my way, a demand to which they all kindly acquiesced. The way I was looking at them seemed to have a persuasive effect. I imagine they just wanted this argumentative; no smoking, stressed out, frazzled, scared of flying weirdo to go to sleep, or Hell, or both. In a bid to relax I began to think about what awaited me under the Caribbean skies. I was staying with a family. I was not going to be holed up in a luxurious hotel. I was going out to see 'real' Jamaicans and the 'authentic' Jamaica. I wondered what they might be like, what their lives had seen and how they viewed their country.

As I pondered on this in a mellow mood, I started to watch the TV again. There were 19 channels, but I was transfixed by one channel, Channel 18. It had a little cartoon drawing of a plane flying between the UK and Jamaica. Then there was the friendly weather and temperature statistics. This was followed by further reassuring statistics regarding the length of the journey and the speed at which we were travelling; so far so good.

Then they showed the altitude at which we were flying.

ALTITUDE?! I don't want to know the altitude! What is the altitude anyway? I know when it changes it means there's something wrong! I was glued to that screen for six hours alternating between calm and panic at the various undulations the little plane made, until much to the relief of the rest of the passengers I finally drifted off to sleep. An hour later, and we had landed.

Chapter Two

Welcome To Jamrock

Montego Bay Sangster Airport is like most airports. Absolute chaos and utter pandemonium wrapped into one crazy little bundle. Having touched down with consummate ease, the best landing this flying-phobic has ever had, there was the usual scrum for bags from the overhead lockers as the first wheel touched the ground. Then the mad dash to be first out of the plane, first through passport control, and all to ensure that the wait for your baggage is just that little bit longer. The way of the 21st Century traveller continues to confuse me. Having collected my luggage and breezed through customs (I got through before FAT FOOTBALL HEAD for the fellow petty minded amongst you), I was then accosted by a uniformed guy who moved all my bags from one trolley to the next and frogmarched myself and the trolley outside to where I hoped my greeting party was.

I was unaware that this act of transference would cost me but then this was the first salutary lesson of being in Jamaica, virtually every physical movement made on your behalf is for sale. This is completely understandable in a country consumed by poverty except for the very hard-working, the lucky, or the corrupt. For someone known to do "The Big Issue" slalom in record time (I give, but when and to whom I want) it will be interesting to see how long I remain conscious of this fact.

Given I was staying with my adopted family, I expected a representative to be waiting at the airport. Instead, I got practically the whole bunch, and what a beautiful and warm welcome I received. The first thing to say about my family is that the names I call them by are, often, quite different from their names given at birth. This is, quite simply, a Jamaican thing. And it is, quite simply, bloody confusing. And so it was that having bump fisted and hugged them all; the four adults, Ras Kelvin, DeeDee, Poochie, and I, and the four children; Mo, Snoop, TJ, and Kaydee, bundled into a Toyota wagon which was custom made for such a bounteous cargo.

I was given the shotgun position next to my dreadlocked driver, Ras Kelvin, whose first action after welcoming me to Jamaica was to ram a thick, juicy spliff into my open mouth. My mouth was open because the journey from Montego Bay to Pleasanton is one filled with incredible wonder. The first item of note was the heat. It is a damp form of warmth which acts as a coolant compared to stifling heats I have encountered elsewhere. As such it is sumptuous. The drive from the airport took me east along the coast towards Ocho Rios, passing through the parishes of Trelawny (my fellow Welshmen have been here) and St. Ann. Other names on the business signs that cluster the coast road briefly took me home. Swansea was there, as was that bastion of 'Posh Essex', Epping. The second most noticeable sign of the kind of society Jamaica is, was symbolised best by the juxtaposition of properties along the coast. Tiny shacks built of flimsy wood and brightly painted struggle to be noticed beneath the awesome and vulgar monstrosities that are sprouting up to cater for fat Westerners who simply can't be arsed waddling around the rest of Jamaica when they can have all the food and drink (and sometimes sex) they desire, all in one place, and all of the time. It might be interesting to see the expression on their faces when they open their ornately decorated verandas, and observe just 400 yards away, people living in abject poverty.

I bet it barely registers.

Armenian Ethiopians

Another early sign of interest was the pace, both pedestrian and vehicular. It is not quite as laid-back as various adverts of stereotype would have you believe, but it sure ain't heart attack inducing. The walking pace is a quarter of that of your average business pace in say New York or London, and more importantly, it is walked with style! The shoulders swing, the arms weave, the feet pad, and the hips groove. If you have seen the movie *Rockers* you will know of the *Stepping Razor* scene where all the main characters are just filmed walking, all with their own distinct style. Gregory Issacs is the best for me, but then I'm biased by virtue of our shared Christian/surname.

This might be a good juncture to introduce myself in a little more detail. Welsh born of Armenian descent, I was first introduced to Jamaica via the beats of reggae and more specifically, the enthusiastic championing of the genre by John Graham Mellor, better known to the wider world as Joe Strummer of The Clash. Born in Ankara to an Anglo-Armenian father, he and I share DNA and an outlook on the world borne of our shared ancestry. Suspicious of authority and victims of genocide and violence for centuries, Armenians side with others whose history is similar to theirs. It is perhaps no wonder then that the history, culture and people of Jamaica have attracted at least two part Armenians to their magical island. Film director Alex Cox, when writing Strummer's obituary, noted that the lead singer of The Clash hated injustice of any sort and put that down to his Armenian ancestry. The Clash visited Jamaica in the later 1970s, an experience put into song on *Safe European Home*. They were produced by Lee Scratch Perry and covered Max Romeo's *Police and Thieves* and Willie Williams' *Armagideon Time* amongst others. Reggae was also influential in their own compositions, most notably on *Guns of Brixton* and *White Man (in Hammersmith Palais)*. More independent musical research led me into astonishing discoveries in the unique wonder of Jamaican music from the 60s, 70s and beyond. There are further links between Armenia and Jamaica, since both the Armenian Church and the Ethiopian Church with its close links to Rastafari are two of the six Orthodox Churches. Indeed, one of the revered texts of Rastafari is the 14th Century Ethiopian epic The Kebra Nagast which introduces us to the first speaking voice thus;

"Gregory, the worker of wonders and miracles, who was cast into a cave because of [his] love for the martyrdom of Christ and suffered tribulation for fifteen years", said, "When I was in the pit I pondered over this matter, and over the folly of the Kings of Armenia, and I said, In so far as I can conceive it, [in] what doth the greatness of kings [consist]? Is it in the multitude of soldiers, or in the splendour of worldly possessions, or in extent of rule over cities and towns? This was my thought each time of my prayer, and my thought stirred me again and again to meditate upon the greatness of kings. And now I will begin."

This Gregory is Gregory the Illuminator, the patron Saint of Armenia who was imprisoned in Khor Virap, a site I have also visited so maybe it was the natural mystic that Bob Marley spoke of that influenced both Joe Strummer and I to investigate more the mysteries, links and wonder of Armenia and Jamaica's people, music and culture.

A further link lies with Ethiopia's Arba Lijoch, forty orphan-survivors from the Armenian Genocide who had found their way to the Armenian monastery of St. James in Jerusalem in 1922 and formed a musical ensemble. When the Crown Prince Ras Tafari of Ethiopia visited Jerusalem in 1924 he asked Armenian Patriarch Yeghishe Turyan if he could bring them back with him to Ethiopia. The future Hailie Selassie took them back to Ethiopia with him and they became the official orchestra of the Ethiopian government, and indeed the first Ethiopian national anthem was written by an Armenian. The orphans were to receive salaries, would have a place to stay and would be trained and educated in the Ethiopian palace. The Crown Prince of Ethiopia could have hired professional musicians but he decided to bring the Armenian orphans instead. This can be explained by the special relationship between Armenians and Ethiopians before 1924 and this special relationship is obvious if you look at the role occupied by Armenian servants of the Ethiopian court at the end of the 19th and beginning of the 20th century.

But enough of me and my fellow Armenians and back to the equally fascinating people of Jamaica.

I began to notice that a lot of the walking that so captivated me on my first day was being done barefoot. Metres away from the shacks these guys and gals are grooving their way to is the kind of ocean side scenery one can only dream of. These impoverished people live next to something that money simply cannot buy. It is almost as if the powers that be, both home and abroad, the powers that could help feed and clothe these people with ease, have an attitude that says, "You've got a lovely view, what the hell are you complaining about?"

My reverie was brought to a shuddering halt, as was the Toyota. We had stopped at a little shack.

"You wanna drink?" asked Ras Kelvin.

"Sure" I replied.

"What do you want?"

"Er, Coke?", I asked.

"You're on vacation man...have something a likkle stronger...Red Stripe?" laughed Kelvin.

"Guinness?" I stuttered.

"Hot or cold?"

"Hmm, I have never had a 'hot' Guinness" I thought and following my travel mantra of when in X country do X country things, I decided to live the Jamaican experience to the fullest and I plumped for a hot one.

"Hot please" I replied excitedly.

On its arrival into my sweaty palm I was somewhat disappointed to discover that a 'hot' Guinness is simply one that has not been in the fridge. I guzzled it down, nonetheless.

"Shit" I thought, "I am going to be stoned and pissed before I even arrive at my destination".

After an hour or so of the coastal drive, all the kids were asleep bar one, and we began to move up into the hills. Ras Kelvin had smoked weed constantly, except for the occasional Babylon road check (Babylon are the police here and they have a vicious reputation, well deserved). He had done so with no apparent effect or impairment to his driving ability. Weed or not, these places have a real hint of mystery about them, as do the roadside vendors who appear sporadically and dramatically on the many twists, turns, and corners that must be navigated. This is the Jamaica I wanted to see, and I was drinking in the sweet sights and sounds. Trees everywhere were laden with exotic fruits; vultures locally known as John

Crow circled the dramatic skies, whilst tiny shacks crowded beneath a canopy of natural gorgeousness. The shacks were selling fruit-stuffs, Jamaican T-shirts, Rasta hats and wood carvings, one of which was of a life size Rasta with a semi-erect penis that must have been at least a foot long. Further along were, rivers snaking their way towards a similar destination to us, mountains constantly fighting the clouds for dominance, and huge chunks of green beauty spilling onto roads already shrouded with natural splendour. As we approached the entrance to my destination, the town of Pleasanton, and having already passed through Walkers Wood and Moneague, I considered that I could write a book on this journey alone. It is quite something.

On exiting the van, I took the opportunity to stretch every inch of me that had been squeezed into a car; a plane, a car, for the best part of 12 hours. I was in Jamaica, and I was at my home for the next four weeks. Time to relax. Two things were instantly noticeable about the house I would be calling home. First, there were the huge gates that many properties feel are required in today's sometimes violent Jamaica. That violence has a history. Jamaica was discovered, and prospered through the use of disgusting, criminal violence reaching its stomach-churning apogee under the slave system introduced by the British, hence those town names I had seen. Today still, the various political parties utilise this old fashioned yet influential and powerful tool to ensure their own prosperity is maintained. Another reason for violence in Jamaica today is poverty, and when violence is being used against you, then it is understandable that it will be used by the victims also. Bob Marley succinctly noted this when he sang, "A hungry mob is an angry mob".

As it happened, food was high on my mind at this point too, having not eaten (if it can be called that) since being a guest of

Richard Branson. Before I could get food however, I couldn't help but wonder at the second noticeable thing about 'my' house; the splendour of the garden. It was like a mini-Jamaica! Flowers and fruit peeked out from beneath a blizzard of fantastic colours. As I climbed the steps of the house, I first met Buzzy and Radar, two extended family members who were just chilling in the yard and self-consciously looking cool, and then I was introduced to Kaddy and Jay, DeeDee's other children who had not been able to fit into the van. Finally, I was greeted warmly by the matriarch and patriarch of my family. Momma greeted me with a huge hug and kiss and a "Welcome to Jamaica!" whilst Pops stuck out a firm hand and said, "You're here at last!" It felt like that too, as if I had always been destined at some point to arrive here and I was thrilled at doing so.

Momma then asked the best question I had heard all day, (better than the second to last question I had been asked, that being "Did you pack these bags yourself?", normally uttered in a dull uninterested monotone because they know your answer already, as readily as they know they will be rifling through your underwear and personal effects within the next twenty seconds), "Do you want to eat?" And so it was that I sat down to dinner surrounded by fellow eaters and an interested party of spectators. I was given sweet potato, plantain, a beautiful vegetable mixture, and some chicken which I wolfed down. Despite it being offered, I passed on the chicken neck, especially given that for this trip and for ease I had decided to be a lapsed vegetarian and that in my semi vegetarian state I considered it one part of a chicken too far. Maybe I will return to my roots so to speak. Pops and I chewed the fat, not the neck; I was given a drink, and then this sprightly and good-looking pensioner (I just know he was a 'rude boy' back in the day) conspiratorially asked me to follow him. We went into a back room from where he produced a black normal sized plastic shopping bag.

"This is for you for your stay", he announced. He then unwrapped the bag and inside was approximately a quarter of a pound of weed.

"I got it from a friend" he laughed, "and I thought you might like it". Jamaican generosity is another thing of wonder, I thought.

I asked how much it cost. He said he bought it for "Not much, about $500...Jamaican".

That worked out to be approximately $5 US and three of your finest English pounds. I asked if that was a friend discount, but Pops explained it was the going rate. I now understood the appeal to those of a criminal persuasion in the Western world of doing business with Jamaica. Meanwhile Pops was giggling at the irony of it all. What a shame that the one thing that the West desires from Jamaica is against the law. Imagine if its export was legalised. Imagine what Jamaica could be with a trade in this controversial drug, a drug that does less harm than alcohol and a drug that if you are a believer, is God given. Poverty on the island could be eliminated. Anyway, Pops rolled me a conical masterpiece and we ventured out into the yard. The male population of this fantastic family began to 'reason' and shoot the breeze, whilst I became, rather too quickly, totally, and utterly stoned.

I looked around my new family. Ras Kelvin is an extremely tall, gangly man, his height extended by the impressive head wrap he wears. He is of the Nyabinghi order of Rastafari. (There was some initial and dangerous confusion amongst everybody when I asked what sect he belonged to. I was misheard at first and to them it sounded like "What sex are you?" much to my embarrassment and their amusement). I had already noticed that he smoked a prodigious amount of ganja and decided it would be folly to try and keep up given I was already semi-comatosed. Kelvin's partner DeeDee is short of stature, but contained a quiet authority and is mother to Jay, a sporty but quiet teen; Kaddy, equally quiet, and "margar" as they say round here when someone is very thin, Mo who is much younger and is mostly quiet except for when he is playing with TJ, which is when shouting becomes de-rigeur. The latest addition to DeeDee's brood is Kaydee, a beautiful little girl who like her mother seems to take in everything with a quiet but observant demeanour. Real authority comes in the form of Momma, who is everything one expects of the matriarch of a big family. She is a bundle of fun and seriousness, alternating between the two within the space of seconds. In any room in which she is standing, she dominates. The children in the family do not, ever, EVER cross her. When Momma says "Jump", these kids try to break the Olympic record. Yet she is an incredibly warm and passionate woman. Her husband Pops is a sprightly pensioner whose whole being denies the years he has been on this planet. He walks and talks like someone twenty years younger, and he speaks the language of fun. Poochie is the mother of Snoop, a tall and athletic fifteen-year-old, who, in a family that contains several quiet members, out-quiets them all. He has another name that reflects his personality; 'Bones', being short for 'Lazy Bones'. TJ compensates for Snoop's silence with regular bouts of hyperactive chatting, mostly 'fart' as they say in these parts. Poochie, lithe in stature, is like DeeDee, an observer but she has the loudest laugh of all and is a teller of the most fantastic stories. Radar and Buzzy are typical mid to late twenties men. They revel in fun and women. Radar is stocky and well built, whilst Buzzy is wiry and sprightly, and both seem like real gentlemen...especially to the ladiessssssss.

Pleasantown

After our meal we went for a walk down the street and on noticing an upcoming group of people, I suddenly became aware that I was carrying half a joint and a bottle of Red Stripe. As well as thinking what a stereotypical fool I looked, being white in Jamaica carrying half a joint and a Red Stripe, and having a touch of weed induced paranoia I considered that this could be some bizarre looking bust party from the local police station.

"Damn, should I hide this?" I whispered to Poochie.

Her response was quick. She laughed at me.

The final event of the night was the bedroom, unpacking. You might not consider this an event, but believe me, it is an astonishing spectacle. The family as one flew over my bags whilst I fielded a barrage of questions and instructions about where things should and would be placed. Within seconds I had unpacked! It was amazing, and I do make it sound a little too easy, but it was like a military operation of precision.

Now I happen to consider the patois that all members of this family speak to be a fantastic and creative language; it is musical, it is Old Testament, it is positive but it sure is hard to follow. The reason for this is due to the number of abundant, redundant words that are used. I will be following my "chos", my "whas" and my "wha' gwaans" with consummate ease, and then they will end their sentence with a word that is superfluous to the sentence. In the time I am pondering on the meaning of this "dem", "suh" or "seen", whilst not being sure if it was the end of the last sentence or the beginning of the next, the speaker is off on a totally different conversation and I have lost the thread and the plot of what everyone is talking about.

Anyway, now unpacked we all said our first ever "Goodnights" and I went to my room. I paused briefly to fully take in that harmonious, choir-like hum of insects that is a feature of life in this wonderful climate.Then I had my first and much needed shower, and a final cigarette of the day (normal). I closed my door, and then I closed my eyes on an eventful first day in the country of my dreams, Jamaica.

Chapter Three

Keeping It Up In Kingston Town

"Isaac, we are going to Kingston, do you want to come?" Momma yelled up the stairs.

"Of course! What time is it?" I slowly responded.

"Six o'clock! We have to go quickly so we can pick up a barrel."

Ah, barrels. Barrels are a system of export from the diaspora to the homeland and having witnessed a barrel packed in the UK with various clothes and foodstuffs sent lovingly from friends and family abroad I thought it would be interesting to see what happens at the other end.

An early start is obviously necessary. I had a quick mega sweet coffee made by Radar (Jamaican style - condensed milk and sugar), and then we were off. The weather was foggy but as you walked into it the effect was more like an ultra-fine rain. There is nothing like such a sweet and refreshing start to the day. It would not stay that way because the drive from Pleasanton to Kingston is not a simple one. Buzzy, who was driving today, had to navigate a barrage of holes and loose stones in the road by driving from side to side at some speed (which he didn't have to) before we could really get going.

Once we did, the sights were as memorable as they had been on the day of arrival. The lushest vegetation on the planet for as far as the eye can see accompanied us all the way down the mountainside. Every few minutes it was interrupted by the kaleidoscopic colours that make up a roadside house, shack, or store. There is a real vibrancy to the way in which Jamaicans decorate their buildings, thereby matching the nature of the people. The locals were already up and about; walking to work, waiting for the bus, going to school, or simply hanging out. Some were manning stores offering the delights of mangoes, pineapple and guinep (tiny fruits the size of a strawberry that you bite into, remove the outer casing, and then suck on the sweet juice before spitting out the hard centre). I was desperately looking for a cigarette shop so I could begin doing what I do wherever I go; follow my mantra of 'When in X country, smoke as X country does'. This meant that Craven A would be my smoke of choice. I was glad of a relatively mild brand because on a trip to France I thought I'd need a new trachea after two weeks on the Gitanes.

The colours of Rastafari; red, gold and green dominate the man-made vistas and it makes for some striking sites. Some houses are further embellished with portraits of Marcus Garvey and H.I.M. Hailie Selassie and biblical slogans of depth and import to the owner. Many of the commercial outlets have been Rasta-cised too although the depth of the proprietor's devotion might be questioned. Nevertheless, as far as Rastas are concerned, if these people are choosing to make profit from their prophet, then they will get their comeuppance when Jah returns running amok through these shacks of capital and damning their pretend utilisation of the Rastafarian creed in order to make profit. They could of course be what in communist Russia were known as 'fellow travellers', that is they are those who are not card-carrying Rastafarians but ones sympathetic to the ideals. Who knows? Let Jah sort 'em out.

The living standards for the majority are made more apparent on this journey. Poverty rules the roads of Jamaica and in a seeming act of serendipity, one of the tunes that accompanies us on the radio this morning is Morgan Heritage's *Nothing to Smile About*. Morgan Heritage are a little reggae-lite for my tastes (although *Down by the River* is bona-fide classic), but the message of this song is hard hitting. Buzzy told me that the song was written in response to a Norwegian tourist who had obviously fallen for the myth of Smile Jamaica, and who was confused by the screw-face (serious looking) appearance of most of the men he had seen. The Morgan Heritage response is dripping with anger, both at the image given of Jamaica abroad and more importantly the conditions their fellow Jamaicans live in.

One aspect that is never really appreciated in any Jamaican stereotype (weed smoking/gun toting etc) is just how prevalent Christianity is on the island. Jamaicans are bountiful in the presence of God. Spiritual succour and salvation live in the proliferation of roadside churches, all with names like The Miracle Home of Jesus Christ. Jamaicans are very Biblical (or churchical as they might say here), very Christian, and sadly for many they are in need of the kind of psychological relief the Church can offer such is their sorry and impoverished lot in life. If one were to view this from a Marxist perspective, it might be suggested that were it not for the church and its role in pacifying the populace the British may have been driven out far earlier via an island wide rebellion rather than the sporadic attempts to rid the island of an undoubted demonic force. Even today, if Jamaicans did not believe in a God coming to help them, they might realise that it is not fate or God's will that is responsible for the conditions they find themselves in but it is in fact a man-made problem that suits the few at the expense of the many.

My political reveries were brought to a shuddering halt by Poochie barking "Isaac, put on your shades!"

She had noticed the not inconsiderable crow's feet surrounding my eyes as I squinted in the sun.

"But I'll miss the colours!" I protested, and believe me, Jamaica is the most outstanding collection of rich, deep, and emotional colours I have ever seen.

Political strife in Jamaica

The gorgeous deep green is occasionally interrupted by a dash of red fruit, a splash of purple flower, or one of the startlingly coloured roadside shacks that I have spoken of. Jamaica's heart is all colours and any journey into the ventricles is a mesmerising melange of primary perfection.

On the route to Kingston Buzzy cheekily pointed out a locally famous rock formation where the trees create what looks like a vagina from the road. It is known as 'Pum-Pum' rock, yet I couldn't find it...but then that's the story of my life. As we got closer to Kingston via a slideshow journey through St. Catherine, we approached Flat Bridge which was something of an early highlight for me. The bridge is known island-wide because it is a single carriageway over a (very deep) river, and at times cars have 'gone over', whilst at other times it is impenetrable because of floods. However, for me it is iconic because as a young child I remember seeing footage of Bob Marley's funeral and his casket being driven over this very bridge on the route from Kingston to his final resting place of Nine Mile, St. Ann, which made the experience a little bitter-sweet and I could certainly feel a natural mystic blowing through the air when I first saw it. Further down the road as we neared Spanish Town, we encountered more groups of guys hanging out (rarely girls incidentally) and more drivers overtaking scarily and hairily on corners. Driving in Jamaica is not for the faint hearted but nevertheless I was observing with the eye of someone who quite fancied taking on some of these lunatics later on in my trip. Spanish Town, despite having a name invocative of siestas, piracy, and rum, is a notorious region of Jamaica containing several gangs, and the equally notorious Gun Court where all the 'bad men' get tried. The reputation of the town was brought to light by the first piece of graffiti I had seen thus far, which lauded the PNP, the historically left-wing party of the Manley's. Portia Simpson, Jamaica's first female Prime Minister was once the party's leader opposing the Jamaican Labour Party, which ironically is the party of the Right in Jamaica. Typically confusing, and typically Jamaica. For parity, further down the road I encountered one of their home-made advertisements too.

As we began to enter the city of Kingston it became apparent that this was a city that did not take global warming too seriously. The smell of petrol fumes clung to the air and the nostrils as we edged our way into this overcrowded metropolis. What was worse was the level of what I initially thought was smog. You could not see more than 300 yards in front of you. However, on reading the Daily Gleaner later that day, the reason for the smog became (ahem) clearer. The Riverton City landfill in Kingston had caught fire on Monday evening and despite it now being Wednesday the fire brigade was still valiantly trying to put it out. Having finally negotiated the unpleasant sense of driving through a bonfire we arrived at our destination, the docks. This must have been what Liverpool was like in its pomp before the eighties and the Tories finally brought the curtain crashing down on that city's livelihood. Kingston Docks has more life in it than any other docks I have visited. The area teems with comings and goings, shouting, car horns, higglers and hagglers, and the obligatory roadside shacks. It is hugely atmospheric. We were there to pick up some barrels which had been sent from England.

First stop meant Pops, Poochie, and Momma going into a building and sorting out the paperwork. The second stop was identical. Red tape and bureaucracy are the same all over the world. Finally, Poochie and Pops were dropped off at the barrel collection point. Poochie later told me that this process was its usual tortuous self. Firstly, there was no queuing system, so it was Darwinism in practice and those with sharp elbows saw themselves served first. Secondly, it is very much a case of who you know, what you know, backhanders and bribes. As such, Pops and Poochie paid three separate people, three (not insubstantial) separate wedges of cash. They were then asked to empty the barrels and re-pack them before encountering the myriad of motor owners offering to transport their barrels for them. This process took approximately four hours.

In that time, I had a sweet pudding (a grey and unappetising looking slice of cake that is surprisingly tasty and sweet) and some fruit juice with Momma in the Dock canteen, where she told me that a lot of the delay with the barrels is a result of security checks aimed at thwarting attempts to smuggle guns onto the island. After anything to eat I like to have a cigarette, but the dock compound was No Smoking, which was ironic given that everyone was smoking today because of the landfill fire, so I made my way outside. Buzzy called me over and asked if I wanted to go to a bar. Never one to turn down an offer of that sort I followed him into one of the shacks. I was expecting a typical bar or pub, and not what was basically a garden shed. Inside were three slot machines, a tiny bar, and including myself, Buzzy and the bartender, about seven drinkers. Others popped their heads into the bar offering to sell items such as watch batteries and steering wheel covers, but you could not fit many more people in than were already there. As I sipped on my first Red Stripe of the day, I took in the US soap opera on the corner T.V., the plethora of posters covering the walls with dates of upcoming reggae events, and the virtually pornographic Wray and Nephew drinks company posters which rather nakedly suggest that to drink their selections of rum will inevitably lead to increased performance and a chance to pull one of the rather forward-looking ladies on the wall. The use of well positioned tits and well exhibited vaginas to sell a product suggests the Saatchi & Saatchi idea of subtle advertising would not be needed in Jamaica. Macka Diamond and Tanya Stephens, two female reggae singers of note, were smiling from two of the posters (with dignity intact) endorsing their chosen drink, although the tag line on Tanya's was the somewhat suggestive *Will keep you up all night.* One suspects this might be true, but more than likely with your head down a toilet such is the over-proof nature of alcohol here. You can see the fumes hovering over every glass!

After two Red Stripes, Buzzy got the call to say that Pops, Momma, and Poochie's tortuous ordeal was over, so we headed back to the dockside, picked them up, and began the long drive back to Pleasanton. The barrels would follow. Despite my sweet pudding, I was still hungry and was glad when we called in at Juici Patties. Patties in Jamaica are a little like Cornish pasties in England only less stodgy and tastier. I had two cheese patties given my renewed commitment to vegetarianism and they were both delicious and filling. The restaurant was set up like a McDonald's and was doing a good trade. Jamaica still has McDonald's and KFC, but to me Juici Patties seems the far healthier and cheaper option, since patties in Jamaica are about a quarter of the price you would pay in England.

When we got back to Pleasanton, all that was left was to wait for the barrels to arrive which they duly did a couple of hours after us. As with my luggage, my family set to work and within minutes all the barrels were emptied, and all the contents had been distributed to various parts of the house. Included in the barrels were foodstuffs, clothes, toiletries, kitchenware, and had a kitchen sink been hauled out I would not have been too surprised.

My evening meal involved rice and that same gorgeous vegetable mix of yesterday which is sometimes referred to as ital since it is salt free and vegetarian and as the Rastafarian saying goes *ital is vital*! I then took time time out to read the rest of the Daily Gleaner and found that both the paper and the T.V. were mercilessly plugging the Reggae Sumfest, my primary reason for being here and I was beginning to get excited at the prospect of interviewing and seeing the performances of some of these artistes. I was now hoping that Tanya Stephens would be appearing so that she might be able to help explain the benefits of her chosen beverage. Just as I was ready to close the day, Ras Kelvin arrived from work. His employment is centred on wood carvings, predominantly of a Rasta theme. I asked if he had made the carving of the Rasta that I had seen on my way up to Pleasanton on my journey from the airport. This aroused quizzical questions from the rest of the family as to what I was talking about. Ras Kelvin explained that I was referring to "big bamboo man", much to the merriment of everyone. Ras Kelvin's carvings however are far more spiritual in nature. There were incredible depictions of lions, a footballing Rasta, sea mammals, walking sticks with ornate designs, and a carving of a moon and the sun coloured with the red, gold and green of the Rasta faith. Ras Kelvin gave me the latter as a gift and within seconds had carved *To Isaac, From Ras Kelvin, Jamaica* onto the back of it. I was deeply moved and for a cack-handed, failed school woodworker who cut himself more than the wood, I was astonished by his skill with a chisel. He then gave me a wrap of weed as a further gift (like I needed it) and I was once more overwhelmed by the generosity of these people. Jamaica, and more importantly its people, were everything I could have possibly hoped for. It is amazing that in these corners of the world where people don't have much by way of necessities, their giving nature is so large. In the West where we have everything we need and so much more, we cling to it covetously and put laws in place to prevent others getting it. If only there was a way to take the best bits of every society and put it all together across the globe, we could live in an atmosphere where we all have what we need and where we are encouraged to share and be generous with our possessions.

And that would be just *irie*.

Chapter Four

All Roads Lead to Ochi

Having travelled to Kingston the previous day where the likelihood of seeing a British tourist was minimal, especially down by the docks, it seemed only right that I venture to the other extreme with a trip to Ocho Rios (or Ochay Reachus as the locals say - or amongst my family the shortened Ochi). The purpose of this trip was to visit the 'big' supermarket to get supplies in for my stay. If you see pictures of Jamaica and there is a huge cruise ship in it, it will almost certainly be Ocho Rios, as it is the favoured stopping point for Brits and Yanks alike.

"All Roads Lead to Ochi!" bellowed Momma as we set off. Radar was driving today, and the way he swung the steering wheel around and the speed at which he drove made me crave for the statelier driving of both Ras Kelvin and Buzzy. We moved through Pleasanton and onto Moneague, passing a building site where I was shocked by the hive of activity taking place. There was no-one sat down reading the newspaper over a crafty cig and a cup of tea like in the UK, these boys were grafting. I have never seen such an industrious building site, and there wasn't an arse cleavage in sight either. We drove on and bumped into Buzzy who was returning from the shops. On hearing that we were going to Ochi, he decided he was going too and joined us for the journey, but sadly not at the steering well. Then Buzzy spotted a family friend, Michael the mechanic, so we stopped to chat and some more introductions took place. While they conversed, I looked out of the window and wondered once more at the sheer COLOUR of it all. In Pleasanton, no-one wears grey. All the clothes shine and shimmer, and the buildings are such an uplifting sight first thing in the morning that Jamaica positively dazzles. Once we had finished our chat, Momma bellowed "All Roads Lead to Ochi!" once more and we were off again. Only we weren't. After 40 or 50 seconds we stopped again, this time outside a salon so Poochie could book an appointment. When she got back into the car Momma once more yelled "All Roads Lead to Ochi", and this time they did.

As we drove down the mountainside, I noticed about twenty vultures or John Crow as they are known locally, circling the sky. The vultures are named so after a particularly fiery preacher who used to go red in the face whilst sermonising and he would open his cloak as if it were a wingspan. It is a murderous sight given that it seems to carry with it a portent of death. As if to confirm this Radar murmured ruefully "Someone gonna die...". He was not referring to his driving, but to the ominous sight above our heads. It seemed like I had stumbled across a bird to rival the magpie in its level of superstition.

For me, that was unfortunate since I am superstitious enough to wave at magpies to ward away the bad luck. This sometimes has a problematic effect, especially when in a car or place of work, or indeed anywhere other than in the privacy of your own home.

"What are you doing Isaac?"

"Err just waving at the birds".

I haven't always done this. I just used to tot up the total and rehearse the rhyme "one for sorrow, two for joy, three for a girl..." until a friend told me that to cancel the curse you must wave at them. As a result, I have been crippled by a need to wave at magpies. Mind you, that same friend and I had already discovered that we have a shared unhealthy obsession with ripping up the plastic stringy bits that come with cans of beer so that birds don't strangle themselves whilst scavenging on bin sites. Maybe if we didn't go through this ritual all the magpies might be killed off and I could live again.

Anyway, back to the vultures.

The sky over which they were circling was punctured by slabs of greenery on which were perched precariously placed dwellings. These beautiful pastel buildings were dotted all over the hillside, and the view they afford is like waking up to paradise. It is amazing to me how man can set up home in some of the most inhospitable conditions; but then I guess the toil must be worth it to know that outside of every window is a chunk of heaven.

The road into Ocho Rios that we were travelling along was the same road that we had come up from the airport on, and so it was that I discovered that the piece of the journey that had captivated me so much previously is known as Fern Gully. As we entered the Gully two tourists were taking photographs of a guy on stilts looking uncannily like the Wicker Man. I imagine that he was representing a sprite or something. I later discovered he was a Jonkanoo, the origins of which are mysterious, but it is potentially an Igbo yam deity embodying the Igbo okonko-masking tradition of southern Igboland, which involves characters in masks of a similar style to that of the quite frightening Jonkanoo masks. Another possible link is with John Canoe who was a heroic king that ruled Axim, Ghana before 1720, the same year the John Canoe festival was created in the Caribbean. Either way, he scared the bejesus out of me. Once my family became more comfortable with me and as I became better versed in patois I noticed I was often playfully referred to as a Jonkanoo when I did something clumsy or stupid (it happened a lot).

Deeper into the Gully and the sweet, damp, beauty of the place was overwhelming. A third of the way through Fern Gully, and the glimpses of sun that had tickled through the trees disappeared and the roads become miraculously wet. This is where you could imagine a Rasta setting up camp, peeking out from beneath the lush vegetation occasionally just to see if Babylon was still out there before retreating again with a disappointed shake of his muddied locks and returning to pray for the destruction of the wickedness outside. If you look hard enough, you can almost see the smoke rising from beneath the trees, and listening carefully you can almost hear the mesmerising, magnificent Nyabinghi drum beats.

The final third of the Gully returns to the hot and dry conditions of the first. It was incredible to go through such dramatic weather changes in the space of yards. Twice! As we came down the hill towards the entrance to Ocho Rios and I saw the familiar stalls, I remembered big bamboo man. He was not alone now. Every stall seemed to have one today of various shapes and sizes but none lacking in THAT department. The piece de resistance was a nine-foot-high Rasta with a five-foot-long penis. Momma began to explain about a court case that had taken place whereby the government had wanted to ban them, but the tourists (for some unfathomable reason) demanded they stay.

As we reached sea level my ears popped as did my dreams of Ochi, because my first impression of Ocho Rios was not good. In the distance was the obligatory cruise ship, whilst a granite behemoth hotel dominated the skyline.

"Upmarket Blackpool", I cynically considered.

However, on turning onto the main drag I was faced with a street that looked like Disney Town on L.S.D. The assault on the visual senses was hard to take in and the noise also cranked up a level. Pinks and turquoise colours battled for the title of campest as I considered that Liberace would have felt right at home here. It looked clean and tidy and *that* walk was everywhere to be seen, as were a smattering of English and American tourists including a pensioner wearing a shirt emblazoned with the legend *England*. Now, the whole premise of my trip was based on a desire to not, under any circumstances, engage with tourists and this particular meeting with them reminded me of the reason for such a strict approach. Why these people need to announce their country of origin to the outside world with tacky t-shirts and tacky baseball caps, I just don't know. The days of slavery are over. There is no British Empire anymore so that t-shirt counts for very little other than to remind Jamaicans that the violence that the English visited upon the island is responsible for the local population's loss of their African surnames, culture, and ancestry. What thought process goes into choosing to pack that for your holiday?

"I will take my England shirt because we are adored all over the world, and I will be treated with the respect I deserve. We built the Empire you know?"

No, you just look like an arsehole.

These days, wearing an England shirt anywhere but England is liable to produce a reaction of contempt, disgust or simply disappointment. That said, by most accounts Jamaicans love England, or at least the prospect of moving there.

As I got out of the car, Bob Marley's 'Crazy Baldheads' was playing on a sound system in the middle of the street. Poochie began to laugh and repeated the line "Going to chase those crazy baldheads out of the town".

Given I am folically challenged, I got the inference.

"They must have seen me coming" I responded.

But here was something else that amazed me. 'Baldheads' was followed by 'War', and people were walking along the sidewalk singing the words for all they were worth. I heard one voice to my left, two to my right, three in front, and one behind. It was beautiful. People were singing along without seeming to have a care in the world. One member of the choir was Radar, who as I was discovering needed little encouragement to sing along to the sounds on the radio.

Anyway, on to business and I needed to change some money. $170 Jamaican dollars was approximately one British pound, so I felt like a Getty when I left the counter. As I sat outside the souvenir shops that contained aggressive salesmen whose demeanour served only to encourage me to shop elsewhere, I noted two things that sum up two key aspects of Jamaica so far. In the first instance I watched an elderly Jamaican, grey of beard, bent double, hobbling up the road on his walking stick. He was dressed in clean linen shirt and trousers, but his shoes betrayed poverty. They were twisted and disintegrating pieces of leather, riddled with holes. As he passed the shop something silver and spherical caught his eye. He dabbed at it with his stick before shuffling off, sighing resignedly. It was a poignant sight in the cash inducing tourist-ville that is Ocho Rios. The second was when I was chatting to Buzzy, only for him to frequently break off from listening to me to murmur "Hey Sweetheart, what you doin' here baby..." and other such sweet-nothings to any good-looking lady who passed him by. Sexuality is something that Jamaicans have in spades, and yet Jamaica is very much a good hearted Christian *gyal*. It seems incongruous that these same people who thrive on the chase and lap up the sexual advertisements for all manner of things, are in the majority devout Christians of one strain or other.

My thoughts were interrupted by a very serious drama on the pavement outside the shop. Poochie's heel had come away from her shoe. Now this is a very grave situation, as all males will understand. But what happened next could only be the case in Jamaica as Poochie was instantly surrounded by men offering their services. They were practically fighting over themselves to be the one to receive the honour of "*fixing da lady shoe*". It became a race to see who would be the first to return with some glue. The winner set about his task with real determination using two types of glue, one of which was called "Crazy Glue" now famously viral because of an unfortunate American woman using it on her hair. He was working at a furious pace, running streams of glue up and down the shoe before pressing it hard and then lifting it off again because the glue had not set. One guy who I had noticed watching the scene with some amusement on the other side of the street walked past our 'hero', muttering "Hey! Are you a shoemaker now?" before disappearing up an alley. After fifteen minutes, Shoemaker recognised defeat. This immediately led to a further scrum of people offering Poochie new types of footwear. First the type of footwear was decided. It would be sandals. Everyone dashed off in different directions before returning with flip flops of all hues and colours. One particularly persistent salesman was trying to get Poochie to choose between a pair of Tommy Hilfigers and a Jamaican flag set. Poochie asked how much they were.

"5 dollar or 10 dollar" he answered.

How much in Jamaican? She persisted.

"5 dollar or ten dollar" he replied glancing at me and seeing my pale complexion thereby mistaking me and Poochie for being something other than we are.

"Are you American?" he dangerously questioned.

"I am Jamaican!" she replied fiercely, with a look that I am guessing has been passed down the generations and resembles Jimmy Cliff in the bike yard scene of *The Harder They Come* when he cries,

"DON'T FUCK WITH ME!"

Poochie opted for the Jamaican number, and we moved away. I was simply amused and impressed that I had just witnessed a scene akin to that of another brilliant Jamaican film, *Rockers* where they are haggling over the price of a motorbike in such a fashion that it looks set to explode into war.

Driving around Ocho is like walking around Brixton in London. The latter really is a microcosm of Jamaican life. Again, it's in the walk. You could never tire of watching the different variations, although with some of the male variants you begin to think, "He's practised that".

A *Juici Patties* stop was made where I ate chicken I am afraid to say, and then we moved onto the petrol station where one guy was simply standing on the corner dancing next to a sound system. He was not trying to sell anything, he was just having fun. I watched him as we turned the corner just to check it was not an act for the tourist but no, there he was, still skanking. In fact, in Ocho Rios there appears to be a sound system on every corner. It's like the Notting Hill Carnival every day. Also, everyone, everywhere, shouts. In the house, in the car, or on the streets, people bellow to one another. It can be misleading because it sometimes appears to be very aggressive, but is in fact, just the Jamaican way. When the smiles crack out this becomes apparent.

We arrived at the supermarket, which was pretty much like a supermarket in England, pricewise too. It was however refreshingly cool in there. Our shopping spree was long and laborious, as my new family excitedly sought to advise me

Ochi salesman ready to saddle up

what I might like but after initially taking the advice of those gathered, I soon became so confused that I just handed over the reins, my only instruction being "strictly Jamaican" and preferably "strictly ital" (vegetarian and salt free) as I was now beginning to get a handle on the lingo. Everything that was put in the trolley looked exotic and tantalising and I could not wait to try out some of these mysterious wares. On our return journey we ascended the mountain through the Gully once more, and then, just as we hit Pleasanton the heavens opened. I imagined the glee on Pop's face at the thought that his wonderful garden would get some much-needed nourishment. Poochie, now recovered from her wardrobe malfunction, was reminding Momma of the myth of a man who used to live in St. Thomas. This man was a devout Rastafarian, and when it began to rain, he would come out to the front of his porch and yell,

"JAH RASTARARI!"

Then, when the thunder roared, he would once more come to the front of his porch, and thunder himself,

"JAH RASTAFARI!"

Finally, as the lightning took hold, the Rasta would come to the front of his porch, and stand, hands on hips, stock still, moving his head in an angular fashion to show off his various profiles.

When asked what he was doing, he replied grandly,

"Jah a tek mi picture!"

In Pleasanton I was dropped off and ventured into the internet café, whilst the rest of the Ocho Rios crew headed to the salon. The internet café was a strange affair. You climbed up some steps onto a balcony/veranda and through a door into a darkly lit room, in which was crowded about five computers and twenty people. There was lots of laughter as about ten kids were crowded around one computer watching YouTube clips of people falling over, people falling off motor bikes etc. A smaller group was watching what looked suspiciously like an illegally downloaded version of a Will Smith film. I spent half an hour sending out quick emails by which time Buzzy and Radar had returned to drive me the few hundred yards back to the salon. I was more interested in the outdoor bar next to the salon which contained several exotic drinks both alcoholic and non-alcoholic. I opted for a fruit punch and sat with the others watching an old documentary which contained a report on Jesse Jackson making derogatory comments about Barack Obama, who still retains admiration in this country (Cocoa Tea once released a song named after the former President). There was much head shaking amongst those gathered in the bar. Jesse's comments smacked of "should've been me" syndrome. The mood of dissatisfaction with world affairs was soon overcome by the sound of a loudspeaker. Everyone made their way out to the front of the building where a car with a speaker attached to the top was dawdling up the street surrounded by what appeared to be floodlights. I wondered if maybe an election was due and that this was one of the candidates spreading his promises to the rural community. As it got closer, I discovered it was promoting something quite different.

"It is Miss Walkers Wood Parade this Saturday! The best sounds will be there! Come vote for your Miss Walkers Wood!"

At this point, the lights I had seen, all darted from around the back of the car, and eight impressive looking motorcycles took the lead. Each motorcycle carried a male driver, and I presumed, one of the candidates for the title of 'Miss Walkers Wood' on the back. It was a strange spectacle, but a very Jamaican form of promotion. As I returned to my drink, I could see and hear into the salon where Poochie was having Jamaican flags painted onto her nails. I think the comment of the flip flop seller about her being American had really got to her. However, at this juncture they had paused briefly, as the nail painter took out a folded over black plastic bag and unwrapped it producing something further wrapped in newspaper. This was again unwrapped further like a solo game of pass the parcel, and out came a piece of red herring which everyone in the salon began to eat. I couldn't imagine the hairdressers of England downing tools to eat a fish. I could also hear them discussing the upcoming Sumfest, and some of the artists. Jah Cure was mentioned, and words cut across each other as some lauded his music whilst others were commenting on his period of incarceration on a rape charge. Doubts have been cast on his 'Ras' reputation because of his stay in prison. I immediately began to wonder if I should mention this, should I get an opportunity to interview him. However, as this conversation was taking place, another cure was being discussed a few miles away. Pops had noticed that I had a cough that was one of those cold type travelling coughs you get from being cooped up with four hundred people and about four million bugs for nine hours. He had promised that on my return from town he would fix me a remedy. We left what I already considered to be 'my local' and Pop's potion was waiting for me when I arrived back. In a glass was a very small measure of liquid draped over two enormous ice cubes. Its colour was dark green and in fact, it reminded me of bile. It didn't smell too hot either. I took a small swig, and it nearly took my head off. Almost immediately my throat was burning up with an intensity I had never known.

"What's in it?" I croaked.

"It is some really good weed soaked in white rum, man. It will sort you out", Pops replied. I managed to finish it over about half an hour. The (over)proof of the pudding will come tomorrow. After chatting on the veranda for a while, Pops and I went into the kitchen to join in the evening chat. This is another aspect of Jamaican life. It seems that at the end of the day, everyone sits or stands around the kitchen or porch area swapping stories, short and long, myth and reality, truth, and wonder. Momma is without doubt the figurehead of these sessions with her devotional family spread around her. DeeDee the listener interjects occasionally with an incisive comment, but she is also highly industrious and washes the dishes, cleans up, chats and eats, whilst all this is going on, and all with one-year old Kaydee clamped to her side. She, Mo and Kaydee will head back to their own home in Trelawny soon but promise to be up again to see us. The sound coming from the kitchen is one of fun and laughter. It seems to me to be the perfect way to end any day.

Chapter Five

Up in the Hills

Today I was going up in the hills. I had been teased mercilessly about my going into the bush. Apparently, I was going to end up with more mosquito bites on me than a pair of teenage lovers on a first date. I seriously considered wrapping my trousers into my socks, such was the paranoia I was feeling about something getting up *there*. I didn't, but I still looked like a pale imitation of 'the great hunter'. As it turned out, I received more bites before I left than during the entire day in the bush. In the hills I would be far from the tourists and deep into the heart of Jamaica. Pops was taking me to see one of his brothers who lives in the house where he was born and works upon the land on which he was raised.

Our journey began with Buzzy at the wheel, the choice of driver fast becoming like a game of Russian roulette. This was especially the case now that Buzzy was driving like an absolute maniac too (possibly due to the absence of Momma amongst the human cargo), which now meant that only Ras Kelvin could be trusted to get me anywhere at a leisurely pace. Radar was along for the ride, with Pops and me making up the numbers. Driving through Pleasanton with the windows down is like inviting conversation. The air is filled with car horns and greetings of "Wha' up Man?!" Cars stop in the middle of the road to continue their conversations whilst pedestrians wander over to cars, lean in, and make general chit chat. It is like everybody has woken up and is thankful for the chance to be here for another day. The crossroads in Pleasanton is a hive of activity, with everyone passing each other at some point. Every aspect of Jamaica moves through these roads. The joyous salutations give a 'lift' to, what is for many, a very hard

Claremont trade

day, even if it is done at that pace. An elderly woman walks past carrying a basket on her head. There is a commotion outside, so the hairdresser sticks her head out of the door whilst still teasing her client's hair. The men hang around in groups discussing the news with each other, national and gossip.

Today I was moving on a different road aimed up into the heavens of the country. Pleasanton to Claremont is a constant climb and Buzzy battled with other drivers for the best piece of road as we left our home village. We passed by Moneague once more with its Teacher Training College perched on the corner and were almost immediately once again in the wilds. Some of the faces I pass on the road have lived a life. The criss-cross of lines on their faces tells the tale and when it is cupped by a snowy beard and capped by a snowy head the look is one of wisdom personified carrying with it an element of 'dread'.

As we arrived at Claremont I was once more assaulted by the heavy thud of bass laden reggae. Music is a constant theme here and reggae is king as you'd expect and as I had hoped for. In Jamaica, you have a 24-hour soundtrack. Momma and Pops have it playing constantly in the home, it is on permanently in the car, and on practically every corner there are the freshest tunes chiming out. And everywhere, people move to it. It might be the slightest of body movements, but it seems that Jamaicans cannot help themselves. We had only stopped off briefly in Claremont to pick up some pig feed for Pop's brother, but it was long enough for me to get into another scrape. I had got out and was taking some photographs before we moved on. Once the car was in motion again, Buzzy had spotted a security guard with a gun outside a set of convenience stores. He suggested that I take a picture of him as we drove past. I gullibly complied. As the car passed the guard, I whipped out the camera, took aim, and fired. The guard returned fire with a volley of abuse which had my driving companions in hysterics. One of his comments was that I should pay him for the picture. I later discovered that he was guarding the shops whilst security made their collections. Not my wisest moment on the trip.

We travelled further north and the road to Bob Marley's home at Nine Mile was pointed out to me. It is heartening to see that there has not been a super expressway built to Bob's house because this area of St Ann is an unspoilt region of Jamaica. Still we climbed, and I was confronted with the most spectacular vista I had seen thus far; a green canvas dotted with bright oranges and fragrant reds sparked and sparkled in the distance accompanied by cattle grazing beneath a sky that threatened to burn them or soak them but was too laid back to decide. I saw hills and mountains that incredibly and bizarrely followed the laws of symmetry. The air was becoming rarefied as we entered what is real farming country. Suddenly, Buzzy pulled up onto what appeared to be a grass verge, which then miraculously turned out to be the road to Pop's brother's house. A sharp bend, and then there was the most Hansel and Gretel cottage you have ever seen. This was the house in which Pops was born. Inside were small and cool rooms plastered with Christian memorabilia and a simple TV

Bensonton

set. I always find it fascinating to meet people like Pop's brother because wherever you travel to across the globe, farmers who toil in remote locations always have a demeanour perfectly suited to their environment and the nature of their work. Pop's brother looked like a tough, serious, and hard man. We dropped off the pig feed and then Pops gave me a tour of his brother's garden. There were two cows nursing their one-week-old offspring. A timid pig was tethered in a corner and despite the fact he appeared to be trying to run away he looked like he wanted to kill me in the same instant. There was also a magnificent garden in which anything and everything was growing including delicacies and Jamaican staples such as yam and breadfruit. Pops called me over to the furthest reaches of the garden where there were some magnificent weed plants, eight feet high. He told me to touch them so I could take in the smell off my hand even though the odour was already overbearing. I did so, and it smelt refreshingly sweet, not like the sometimes-sickly odour you occasionally get. To celebrate Pops pulled out a fat joint and passed it to me. I did what comes naturally. The rest of the garden was a nature lover's nirvana. Flowers of every conceivable colour festooned the place along with exotic plants of such height and arrangement that they appeared to be outside palaces.

Then, almost miraculously, I gained my first sighting of Jamaica's national bird, the Doctor Bird. Not one, not two, but several of them, all fizzing their way through the garden nectar. Green of plumage and effervescent in nature, the colours on the bird positively shine from its darker hued tail all the way up through its glittering emerald feathers to its red elongated beak. I have never seen such a fantastic looking bird; in fact, I am unsure if I have ever seen a hummingbird before, so this was a glorious introduction. The garden also contained two grand monuments to mark the spot where Pop's mother and father are buried. Jamaicans used to be able to bury their family in their own gardens but apparently a law has been passed preventing it. I think it is a lovely idea for the bereaved partner to be able to spend what time they have left with their loved one. I would want to be able to sit out and talk to my life partner and love each day. Where is the harm in that?

We walked back to the house and Pop's brother had kindly packaged up some corn on the cob for me...that Jamaican generosity again. We bade our farewells and moved down the road to a mysterious and not particularly well know site of interest, a place known locally as Hutchinson's Hole. This place became infamous when a Scotsman arrived in the 1760s to look after the Edinburgh Castle Estate. Local legend has it that Lewis Hutchinson kidnapped passers-by, decapitated them, robbed them and threw their remains down the hole. Some accounts have suggested that he fed on the blood of his victims, and he was also known as the Mad Doctor. He is estimated to have killed over forty victims before he was captured whilst trying to escape at sea, and eventually hung. No bones have ever been found. Is this Jamaican fact or Jamaican fiction? Whilst quite possibly mythic, upon searching his home after his arrest, approximately 43 watches and a large amount of clothing was found so who knows, but it's a cracking story.

From a distance the hole looks impressive, but the closer you get the more sceptical you become as it seems to reduce in size as you near it. My judgement may however have been impaired by an incident just minutes before. Pops was leading the group down to the hole, and let me tell you, Pops can shift. Being Welsh born, I pride myself on my ability in the mountains and yet I was conscious of not going over on my right ankle, something I do regularly now as the result of an overzealous football tackle I once made. Unfortunately, I soon discovered that my descent would have been perfect if only my footwear was compatible with the sodden rocks, but it wasn't, and so I went arse over tit smacking my hand; my back, my forearm and one calf on the numerous rocks that had been kind enough to break my fall. I got straight up of course and shrugged my shoulders and carried on like nothing had happened, all the time thinking, "That bloody well hurt". My pride had also taken something of a battering. I realised that now was the time to strip myself of the self-imposed honour of Mountain Goat Order No. 1.

I blame the weed.

When we got close to the hole, we all peered in with a sense of trepidation. I was not that impressed, until Radar threw a rock into it, and we could hear it falling for almost thirty, sinister, seconds. We all had a go, using stones and rocks of different sizes and each time waited an interminable amount of time to hear them land. If there are bodies down there, they aren't coming up any time soon.

Then it was back in the car, a little gingerly for me, to travel up to Bensonton. We had hardly moved along a road scorched by the midday sun when Buzzy again shuddered the car to a halt and everyone got out. To our right was a half-built wall the size of Jericho's; and on the top, up the sides, and along the bottom, was an army of locals all buzzing with activity. Buckets of concrete were being flung about with dexterity and ease and everyone was busy doing something. Very few on the building site were wearing shoes, and none wore a hard hat. Health and safety? Pffft. Pops, Buzzy and Radar all knew some of the workers. Buzzy was asked for a couple of cigarettes and scaled the wall in astonishing fashion to give these to his friends. Radar was doing the same although thankfully he had decided to use the ladders rather than copying Buzzy's Spiderman impression. Meanwhile a smiling youth came up to Pops to ask for money. It was Pop's nephew.

"I come up and down this hill twenty times a day, and every time I pass, the yout' ask fi money!" Pops laughed. The weather was scorching, and these workers were unbelievably industrious in such a climate.

After ten minutes or so of chatting, we got back into the car and drove on for another mile, where, incredibly, the rain was torrential. The way this climate fluctuates is a wonder in itself. Pops had brought me here for the view because at the entrance to the town sits the local school of Bensonton from where the scene is a dramatic landscape of valleys and houses tucked away behind the hulking vegetation. The extra mile was worth it. When we passed the now rain battered Wall of Jamaica again, there was not a soul in sight. I looked back as we turned the corner and given the lack of health and safety regulations being enforced, I was glad to see that the builders were all sheltering under a blue canvas to the back of the wall.

We were heading back to Pleasanton now, but not before dropping in on some more of Pop's relatives. Mr. Hedges is a local schoolteacher, and I was keen to find out what conditions were like for schoolteachers in Jamaica. His niece Elisabeth, who like Mr. Hedges was sat watching the world go by on the porch, is also in the teaching profession. Also present was a sullen looking yout' sharpening a machete and a cat that appeared to be totally stoned. There were about three different conversations taking place on the porch all accompanied by the low-level reggae soundtrack from inside the car where Radar had remained. Often, it was Radar's voice that was leading the singing.

Mr. Hedges was explaining the examination system for pupils and the wage system for teachers and the average teaching wage appears to be minimal and certainly not a great deal to live on given my recent trip to the supermarket. As he and I were chatting serious matters, the sombre tone of the discussion and peaceful surroundings was punctured by Elisabeth yelling,

"I'm old enough to be your mother!"

It seemed that Buzzy was up to his tricks.

"Nuh man, I am 29", Buzzy lied to his 34-year-old prey.

She sighed, sucked her teeth, and then said "OK, show me yuh driving license!"

Buzzy rummaged around his pockets, pulled out a card, and flashed it quickly to his prey. She tried to grab it, but Buzzy was too quick, laughing.

"Man, you want every t'ing from me!"

"You're not 29."

"I am! Born in 1989, it's 2018, do the maths, I am 29!"

Elisabeth was having none of it.

"Cho!" Buzzy resignedly cussed, having realised he was going to get nowhere.

"You're thirty, but you galang like you're fifty!"

Pops decided that Buzzy had had his chance and that it was time to move on. And so we did, back into Claremont. Buzzy and Radar, neither of whom could be described as hirsute, wanted haircuts and so it was that Pops and I got to do that most satisfying of Jamaican customs. We went and ordered a beer from a bar at the hub of Claremont activity, and then stood outside, beer in hand shooting the breeze and watching the world go by. When I returned to planet Claremont, I began to become aware of the sounds. The clip clop of flip flops is everywhere. A concrete truck was roaring through the high street with two girls perched at the front of the hold, one either side, directing traffic and pedestrians alike. The pace is loose, the vibe is good, and fortunately the security guard I

'shot' earlier that day was nowhere to be seen. The local drunk was though.

At about 5ft 2 in height, this ancient little Jamaican man was sprightly, cheerful, annoying and wrecked. He approached Pops and me and made a play for my beer. Pops shouted at him:

"That's not your beer, buy your own!"

It was clear this guy could not afford a beer but it was also clear through his drunken patois brogue that he spent every penny he got on the stuff. After a period of constant badgering, to-ing and fro-ing, and further attempts to grab my beer, Pops gave the man fifty dollars. He returned with a glass with some form of spirit in it looking so very pleased with himself. However, he then made one of his frequent erratic hand and arm gestures and proceeded to pour his valuable liquid all down himself. He looked crestfallen. He shuffled back into the bar no doubt aware that he could not ask us again for money. To our surprise, he emerged once more from the bar with a bottle of Pepsi.

"Now that's what you should be drinking!" exclaimed Pops.

Some things are more upright than others - Claremont

Pleased with his purchase he bumped our fists just as Buzzy arrived back from his haircut. Our new best buddy sensed fresh blood, but on making the slightest of movements of his arm towards Buzzy he was met with:

"DON'T TALK TO ME!"

Buzzy's glare made it clear that this was a non-negotiable request. I am going to try it when I am back in England. It wrestles control from the drunk and puts you in a strong position from the off.

Suddenly, another guy bounced up in front of me. "Remember Me?" he asked. "I'm Bob Marley", he announced before bouncing off down the street. How weird.

Once Radar had returned from his haircut, apparently it is a Friday tradition for the boys, we slung our way out of Claremont and headed back to Pleasanton. I had one more visit to make though. Pops has a friend named Keith who keeps chickens, and I was told that he had a wonderful garden. When we pulled up outside Keith's, I have to say that I was under-whelmed. The front of the house looked like a bungalow and so I did not hold out too much promise for what was behind it. However, as with several things in Jamaica, a conventional façade often hides the most wondrous of truths. As we moved around the side of the house, I was first confronted with a rickety garden shed but behind it was a bona fide tropical rainforest. We walked through it like we were in the Amazon, Keith with cutlass in hand, and me with my head in 'Secret Garden' territory. Within its midst was a chicken coop with three hundred chickens as inmates but this was most definitely Category C as far as prisons go. The hens looked happy and had plenty of space in which to go about their pecking and clucking. Their neighbours were five pigs: one adult and four piglets. We left this happy family and moved deeper into the Amazon. Keith then cut two huge pieces of sugar cane with his cutlass, the same height, and packaged them up with some more corn, and a jackfruit. Keith had said he needed to go to sleep but it was only four in the afternoon. When Pops asked why he was so tired, Keith flung a baleful glance in the direction of the chicken coop.

"Yuh cyant sleep when dey want to see yuh", he responded.

Keith then engaged in a little bit of shadow boxing to limber up for God knows what and handed the corn to a woman who had appeared at the window.

"Miss Smith, can you wrap these for me please?" he asked courteously.

Miss Smith was a sharp, bright, and dainty lady, who also happened to be Keith's wife. It is an engaging aspect of Jamaica that some of the language is from a different, long - gone, more polite age. Older friends call each other Mr and Mrs So and So and rarely use Christian names with each other, and in shops and markets customers are referred to as "Sir" and "Miss". It is a quaint reminder of how society used to be, before the language of guns, knives, carjacking and stealing became the mode of conversation.

Indeed, the Jamaican language is a thing of real beauty and originality. For instance, everyone knows certain Jamaican phrases such as 'cool man' and 'irie', but one I had never heard before was "EEEEEEEEEEEEEEEEEEE!"

This is uttered with mouth stretched and teeth bared, and the higher the pitch and volume, the better. It has a myriad of meanings, from "Yes, I know", to "You're joking?" You could listen to a conversation all day and still be transfixed, and I frequently was.

When we finally returned to Pleasanton, I was incredibly tired. The slightest of exertions can takes its toll in this heat. I sat down for some wonderful food, chicken and pumpkin soup with dumplings. It was just what I needed and wanted but after taking my third mouthful, Momma commanded:

"What's that?"

I looked to where she was looking which was directly at my bashed-up forearm.

"How did you get that?" she demanded.

I was like a kid caught smoking behind the bike sheds. It was instantaneous but riddled with guilt as my head turned towards Pops looking for help.

An explanation was proffered and responded to with: "Wha' the raaaaaaas are you doing taking Isaac down there? It's not safe. You nuh wanna go to St Ann's hospital do you Isaac?"

I shook my head solemnly. The tirade against Pop's continued. I just smiled in Momma's direction as sweetly as I could.

Whilst I had been in Bensonton with Pops, Radar, and Buzzy, the rest of the family had been focused on the continuing tale of Poochie's pamper. Having had her nails done the day before she had gone to have her hair done before a family audience. However, halfway through the day, the stylist had a dentist appointment in Ochi. Rather than go alone, Poochie and the whole posse went with her to what was a mobile dentist on a bus in a busy street in Ocho Rios. They did not go into Ochi for Ochi's sake. They simply went to accompany the stylist's visit to the dentist. This is community living. By the time they had returned I was again parked at the neighbouring bar and by the time the styling was finished it was almost 9pm. It might seem that I spend a lot of my time at the bar, but it is because I simply enjoyed watching the Jamaican world go by, especially at such a sedate and Zen-like pace. We headed home as a John Crow drifted overhead, which may have been a portent of things to come...

A common saying in Jamaica is "Soon come", which means "I will be along shortly". I was beginning to learn that 'it' rarely does come soon, but that when 'it' finally arrives, 'it' often does so with the biggest smile on 'it's face.

Chapter Six

Paranoia Attacks

He is after me. This is not a good situation. I am in danger.

It began last night with a phone call to Momma from the stylist and thus began this morning's wicked chain of events.

Initially the early morning routine had begun in the usual way as I sipped coffee and reflected on the majesty of the mornings in Jamaica whilst waiting for the rest of the family to discard their slumber and congregate on the porch. One by one they arrived, and the early chat was full of the usual wisecracks and bonhomie, but it changed immediately once Momma arrived.

Conducted in thick patois, I did not fully understand what she was saying but I heard enough to be slightly concerned. This is the land of the machete and cutlass after all, and nearly every man I have seen in the country seems to carry one like we might carry a mobile phone.

I heard "Isaac", I heard "white man", I heard "salon" and I heard "He's said he's gonna chop up the bloodclaat".

Initially I thought my hearing was affected as a result of the inroads I had made into Pop's ganga tree gift this morning. But then I noticed that everyone kept glancing at me in a concerned fashion, and so I tried to get everyone to slow down and explain it to me. It thus became clearer, and it was indeed "not a good situation".

Momma took up the story. She told me the stylist had phoned her up last night and had asked Momma if she could hear the commotion outside her house. There was a cacophony of clattering and screaming which, it materialised, was her boyfriend running a stick continuously up and down her grille and shouting angrily at her, demanding to know exactly what was going on between her and 'the white man'.

As Momma related this story, I could feel my heart sink and the nervous smile erected to brace myself for whatever trouble was about to come, slowly evaporate.

"Shit" I thought, "this man sounds vicious and violent".

Momma continued with the stylist's account of how her boyfriend had suspected that she had a supposed lover, and that said ' lover' was in fact... me. The stylist had explained how her insanely jealous boyfriend had heard rumours on the grapevine, (in Jamaica this particular type of plant is the largest known to man) that she was seeing another man. "What's the problem you might ask?" What does this have to do with Isaac Hye? Well, this boyfriend knew one thing about the "other man", the fact that he was from Europe. The suggestion therein was that the said paramour was white. The boyfriend had passed the salon a number of times over the last couple of days and there had always been a white man there, drinking in the outside bar next door. Maths not being his strong point, he did the sums, and vowed to kill and "chop up the rasclaat" when he next saw him. That "rasclaat" was me, and "chop up" is pretty self explanatory. In my stoned and increasingly paranoid countenance my imigination decided it would be more dramatic to further embellish the definition of "chop up" with the words "and blugdeon beyond recognition".

At this point I was waiting to hear of how the stylist's account was pooh-poohed; and how she had explained the real situation to her psychopathic boyfriend, and how everyone had fallen about laughing, and how it was a story that they would remember throughout their long and prosperous married life.

But Momma stopped. I waited; nothing more looked set to come out of her mouth.

"And then what happened?" I anxiously asked, my voice cracking and my being now reduced to that of the grim-faced daze of a man about to face the executioner.

"Oh, she just said to him "well if that's what you want to think....", and he just stormed off cussing her out".

That was NOT what I wanted to hear. "If that's what you want to think"? Is that all she could come up with? There was a potential murderer on the loose looking for a white man in town, and as far as I knew, I was the only one.

Ever since I got here, I have been plied with potent weed (admittedly administered mainly by myself), and now they throw this trip on me? Me and weed and paranoia are common bedfellows. When I lived on the 18th floor of a high rise block in London I once went back four times to check I had locked the door after having had a smoke.

"Ah well", I brazenly replied, shrugging off the impending danger. "Buzzy and Radar are about. They look as though they can handle themselves" I laughed unconvincingly.

"Buzzy and Radar are not here. They went to a dance last night and didn't come back" explained Momma.

"Double Shit".

This put a dampener on the whole day's planned proceedings. I desperately needed to get to the internet café in town to see how things were progressing regarding arrangements for Sumfest. This was made even more necessary because my Sumfest contact, the fantastic Marcia who had arranged practically everything for me, had phoned earlier in the day to say I needed to check my email.

Given the Jamaican climate, it seemed that a pair of glasses, a beard, and a false nose for the trip into town would simply draw further attention to me. The internet café was slap bang in the middle of everything and given my pallor, it is

The Stairway to Safety

inconceivable that I would not be spotted going in. The idea of my travelling incognito seemed to be further thwarted by the fact that whilst we were chatting about last night's events on the porch and putting together a military plan for my foray out, there were constant interjections by mobile phones all wanting to discuss the stylist's boyfriend and the white man. It seemed that by now the whole town knew the story. In the end it was decided that I would try a different internet café, just on the outskirts of Pleasanton. So, Jay, Poochie and Snoop formed a protective (or funereal) cortege around me and off we moved. I had decided to wear my floppiest sun hat and darkest sunglasses.

We managed to reach the internet café with no reported incident, although 'internet café' was perhaps too grand a word for this establishment. It was a shop with two computers in and a hastily erected wooden partition for a degree of privacy. The cost was almost double to that of the internet service in town, but then that was a small price to pay to avoid being macheted up by a jilted nutcase. After finally getting logged on, a tortuous process, I found Marcia's email which carried with it the good news that I would be conducting an interview with the Minister of Tourism, after the Sumfest. This was good news indeed. It is impossible not to notice that tourism is Jamaica's food and drink, yet it also impossible not to notice that the money made neither feeds nor quenches the thirst of the poor on the island. I hope to address this situation and hope further that he might hold some sway in getting MACHETEMAN locked up before he grabs me and chops me into little pieces.

Somewhat disappointingly, I had no further emails, so I handed control of the mothership over to Jay, who was keen to jazz up his social networking site, upon which he had hundreds of friends who, incidentally, were all female as I nipped out for a cigarette.

As we had arrived at the café, I had noticed a huge marquee, not unlike the circus tents we have in the UK positioned centrally in the middle of a field. As I pulled and puffed on the balcony, I discovered what it was for. From underneath the canopy I could hear the most raging fire and brimstone assault on the parishioners booming across the field through huge loudspeakers. The voice was threatening them with death and damnation, but although I knew these were the words of God being spoken, I knew that they were not being uttered by the Man himself. The voice sounded like a southern Bible belt gospel preacher, and I know that if God returned, with the choice of all the accents in the world with which to speak, George W Bush would not be his preference. He might however choose Jamaican. I was glad the warnings regarding living a good Christian life were so loud, because I hoped that, wherever he was right now, MACHETEMAN might hear of the potential punishment for sin, especially murder. A builder was climbing up the stairs to the café when the preacher hit the peak of his apoplectic rage. "Man, that bwoy hangry!", he mumbled to me, and laughed. This is another feature of the Jamaican dialect. The letter 'h' is removed from some words, but then added to others. For instance, I might go to a farmer to get some 'heggs', but to a stylist to get some 'air'. Similarly, I was asked the other night whether I had "beard". I asked for a repetition because I thought that my beard was entirely visible, and it therefore precluded the need for such a question. Again, I was asked the same. It was only after five or six goes I realised that I was being asked whether I had bathed, which in Jamaica is a three-syllable word.

It was now an hour since I arrived at the internet café, and I had begun a printout of a document which would apparently emerge in the manager's office. I was a little concerned about this. He might read some of my less charitable comments and call the police. I would be slung in a cell, most likely next to MACHETEMAN, and never see the light of day again. It amounted to twenty sheets, but it was still not 'finished' when I was ready to leave, an hour later. I thought I knew of a solution, but the Boss was not about to hand over control of his domain to some amateur. Consequently, I did leave with the whole document, but spread over about twenty-seven pages all containing little extracts on about an eighth of each page.

As we walked back, we stopped off at an isolated shack on the outskirts of town to get some phone credit. Perched on benches were a family; father, mother, and two children. I was off in my own world, checking the streets for MACHETEMAN, when the father spoke to me.

"You ok Man?"

"Cool" I replied, trying to get into the languid flow of the language, but failing because I am too set in my un-cool way.

"I like your flex, man".

"Thanks" I replied, not at all understanding what he had meant.

Having survived the trip to the edge of town, I decided to lie low for the rest of the day, but this was in no way going to assuage my rampant paranoia. Every time a car slowed down as it passed Momma's gate, I had dived beneath the parapet should this be MACHETEMAN come to exact his deadly revenge. I was not calmed by the steady stream of arrivals returning from their day, all chipping in with their version of the previous night's events. Radar and Buzzy had returned, still slightly hung-over. This did not prevent Radar from indulging in the most terrifying description of the stylist's boyfriend.

"Yeah man, he is like a bear; he's a big, big, man (he stretched his arms out to emphasise the size), massive muscles, a very violent man".

What a swine! This must be a wind up.

Still the talk was of 'lickin' up', 'choppin' up' and 'mashin' down', with me as the recipient of these licks, chops and mashes.

Phones were going off constantly and the topic was always the same, Isaac and MACHETEMAN. One of the times Momma's phone rang, her authority was once more illustrated. Momma yelled out "mi phone, mi phone!", but I had already seen that on the 'm' of the first "mi'", Kaddy had bolted out of her chair where she had been peacefully watching the television, and vaulted over to where the phone was, so that by the time Momma had finished her perfunctory sentence, the phone was already in her hand.

It was a relative in New York who had phoned to get confirmation of the stylist story.

I'd gone international.

I was relieved when an impromptu game of cricket began to form on the road outside the house, because it took my mind off my imminent demise and back to why I had first come to Jamaica. It was scenes like this that had played in my mind for years. On the road were about ten participants. To their right was a lush gully, to the left Momma's house. A dustbin lid was the wicket whilst the bowling crease was a stick on the floor. It was no holds barred cricket too, with the ball being launched through the air at terrific speeds, most notably by Buzzy and Jay.

There had been a new arrival at the house that day also. Jonesey was an old family friend who was going to be staying for a few days. He was about six-foot-tall, of good build, and slow and laconic of speech. He had also been in bat for an age. I asked Buzzy why he had failed to remove him, and his reply was,

"Jonesy a good cricketer".

Indeed, you could see in his stance, the way he held his bat and in his fluid strokes that he had indeed been a very good player. Buzzy, who is the fastest runner in flip flops I have ever seen, tried several approaches to remove his friend from the wicket, but all were to no avail.He had roared in off a Joel Garner like run up, he had tried to disguise the slower ball, he had tried spin, he had just thrown it down as hard and as violently as he could, but several times the ball had been dispatched into the steep dropping gully and several times Kaddy had gone sprinting after it, nimbly vaulting the flotsam and jetsam that is loose branches and trees. There was a sort of break for lunch too or perhaps it might be best described as a break for 'lech'. Two not unattractive girls were ambling up the road and were heading straight for the wicket. As one, and with no conspiring, Radar, Buzzy and Jonesy positioned themselves in such a manner that the girls would have to pass right through them. Then they could choose their words of attraction in the hope that they might get some reaction. They got none, so simply shrugged their shoulders and carried on. However, after one final and enormous hit, the ball was given up for lost, and so it was the close of the day's play anyway.

This approach towards the opposite sex got me thinking. It appears that chatting up women is almost an obligatory male pastime and given the number of advertisements in newspapers for things like penis oil and penis cream, all aimed at assisting 'growth', it suggests that sex is very much how a man is measured (ahem) in this country. Similarly, some of the lower-brow newspapers are full of letters pages devoted purely to sexual matters and/or infidelity. All of this suggests that in Jamaica sexual conquest is highly competitive, which is precisely why I am facing a good kicking when MACHETEMAN catches up with me.

The porch was the scene for today's end of day gathering. Momma once more dominated proceedings. Jonesy had not been to the house for a number of weeks now, as he is from the St.Thomas area in the eastern reaches of the island. He began by asking Momma about the whereabouts of a pair of his favourite shoes that he had left on his last visit. It turned out that someone had been round to Momma's house and had commented on how nice the shoes were. Momma's response was befitting of such a generous lady. She had given them away. Rather than be vexed, Jonesey took the news with a shrug of his shoulders and laughed along with everyone else at his misfortune.

Momma meanwhile was looking at what pass for toes on my feet. In a field of very healthy competition, my toes are most definitely high up on my list of worst body part. Momma suggested that I get a pedicure.

"He could go to the stylists and get his gyal to do dem" roared Poochie much to the amusement of everybody else, but not me.

The joke-y manner with which everyone talked about my predicament made me feel a little easier about the whole affair. As with a number of aspects of Jamaican life, little things are made big and I guessed that everyone was having a great laugh at my expense. I too was laughing.

Sort of.

Hell, I might even go into town tomorrow.

That evening, as I was using the laptop, I experienced my first power cut. Everything just stopped with no explanation. Total blackout. My first thought, naturally, was that MACHETEMAN had tripped the lights and was making his move to bring an end to his girlfriend's perceived infidelity once and for all. I was sure I heard a cutlass being sharpened. But then the house which had just prior to the power cut become quiet and tranquil for the first time that day, exploded in a cacophony of laughter and noise. Outside my door, I heard Snoop and Jay creeping about. A loud Poochie-ish shriek confirmed what they had been up to. It would appear that in Jamaica every trial and tribulation is faced with good humour and as far as possible, laughter, whether it be the lights going out, day-to-day struggles...or a guest being stalked by a machete wielding mental case.

Chapter Seven

The Day of Rest

As is becoming the pattern I awoke early, this time at 5am, about three hours before everyone else would be up but at least it gave me the time to recover from my dream of a 15 ft man chasing me through the bush with a plethora of Samurai swords. I opened my laptop and set to work detailing the horror of the previous day that you have just read about, when after an hour or so I received a call from nature. I headed to the bathroom to do the necessary when Fate chose this moment for another power cut to occur. They come without warning. I expected them to happen at times of bad weather, but they rarely arrive when expected, rather whenever they feel like it. As is my habit, I had taken a book in to read whilst my bodily functions did their thang. I was therefore in a pitch-black and in an unfamiliar room, trousers around my ankles, book in hand. The tourist guides certainly don't provide information as to what to do in such a situation. My first act was to stand up and to try to find the toilet roll. Doing this in an unfamiliar house is not recommended. I almost knocked myself out on the shower unit and was inches from removing some important, and in Jamaica, revered anatomical parts on the sink unit at the same time.

As a result of my near castration, I decided to wait for one of two scenarios to occur; the electricity to return, or daylight to come up. The latter saved me from reaching the two-hour mark for my toilet stay. Momma was the first to be heard downstairs, signalled by the radio being turned on and the first thing I noticed today was the different genre of tunes. The first hour consisted not of the usual pulsating reggae beats but of Gospel, and somewhat strangely, Ska-tinged tunes praising the Lord. In the advertisement section of the radio programme, I heard the same promotion time and time again.

"It's hurricane season. Be the first to get your home ready..." rae rae.

I say 'rae rae' because that is what Jamaicans use instead of etcetera. On second thoughts, this is not entirely true. I hear Jamaicans saying etcetera, but they say it "ekt-cetra".

I had forgotten that this was hurricane season and I had now been kindly reminded of the fact that another hazard other than the jilted MACHETEMAN was stalking me. Meanwhile Momma admonished me for the impressive amount of smoking I had already done this morning. Not the weed; that is no problem for this family, just the normal cigarettes.

Things on a Sunday are even more laid back than usual. The problem was that after a lack of activity the previous day, partly due to my self-imposed exile from the madman, I was itching to get out and about. When everyone was up and I suggested the beach they looked at me like I was crazy. But they quite like crazy in Jamaica so I was promised my day at Priory, a public beach near St Ann's Bay. The drive to Priory took us via yet another route, one that was just as countrified as the road into the hills. People were dotted along the route, male and female, walking to who knows where, because there did not appear to be anything for miles. The public buses were running, and we encountered several of them on the various bends in the road, all the same colours; blue, white, and rust and all in the same condition, clapped out and spewing smoke with their own private bundles of life on board.

Bicycle riding is another favoured mode of transport, and the style and make of bikes that the young kids in the streets were riding took me back to my youth. With the UK's obsession with all things retro, these bikes would sell for hundreds of pounds if they were exported home.

Given it was Sunday, there was a smattering of the devout on the roads. A woman dressed in her black Sunday best with an elaborate hat perched upon her head waited for a bus. Further along the road was a young boy, standing outside the Church of the New Testament carrying a Bible almost the same size as himself. Radar was driving us today and was a model of restraint. As we pulled into the Unipet petrol station I realised the reason for his renewed caution. He had very little fuel to burn. Petrol stations in Jamaica, besides having names that suggest they cater for budgies, cats, dogs, and rabbits, are like a throwback to gentler times. Unipet is total service, so you don't leave your car. The station had two girls performing at the pumps. I had my window down as the girl came over to fill up our tank which was on my side. As she was filling the car I suddenly became aware of the most beautiful singing voice I had heard in a long, long time. It was not coming from the radio but was in fact the service station girl who, imbued by the Sunday spirit, was battling the birds for sweetest sound in Jamaica with paeans to her Lord. Having finished filling the tank she simply said "Alrite. Respec'." and on she moved to give the next car a gentle reminder of what they should have been doing, and where they should have been today.

Radar soon returned to trying to break the land speed record. He was explaining that this road was dangerous because you get a lot of trucks on it. Why he told me this I have no idea, because he was certainly driving no slower than on previous occasions. In fact, as we were going around corners, you could audibly hear the tread of the tyre being shredded away. Broken-down cars litter the scorched sides of the roads. Perhaps they met Radar on one of his previous excursions along this highway. Fences are cobbled together with bric-a-brac, and the sidewalks appear and disappear totally at random. It would also seem that almost everyone is a graffiti artist in Jamaica. The wording on every sign on every business looks so iconic. Wenna's Cook and Stop Shop, Bev's One Stop Bar, Aunt Biddy's Ocho Cave Shop, have all been written with an abandon and style that is refreshing, and then surrounded by a rainbow of Jamaican shades so that the effect is even more dazzling. A young girl stood at the end of a driveway dressed in another 'churchical' dress, white this time, swaying and singing to the music in her head.

Speaking of which, Radar was in fine voice again too, although he was by now a little vexed. We had been following a slow-moving vehicle that looked like a safari truck due to its black and white striped plumage. It was a Defender, and I got a very good look at it because Radar almost put us into its back seats. After that narrow escape I observed a truck with a sound system attached to the back on its way to providing a hamlet with some Sunday afternoon entertainment. Then Radar took a corner on the wrong side of the road. Poochie, sat in the back with her sleepy children yelled out, "Radar there are pickneys in the car!", and the crestfallen Radar had to curb his excesses immediately. I took this opportunity to ask Radar why the car horn was used so much in Jamaica. I heard some people using one toot, others two, and sometimes three blasts, and wondered if there was a secret code to the toots (but not the Maytals). Radar said that really the horn was used for two things. One was to warn other drivers you are coming (that's Radar's usage explained then), and the other is to 'hail up' someone you know. This is therefore why in the towns there is a constant cacophony of car horns as everyone says "Hi" to each other without actually speaking. Everyone everywhere seems to use their horn and it seems that everyone knows everyone, everywhere.

This contrasts with the 'First' World which has become a place where we don't know our next-door neighbours and where every new form of entertainment, be it computer games, Ipods, mobile phones, all result in us isolating ourselves into our own little private and impenetrable orbit. There, the man in the street can be ignored whilst the skills of conversation slip into further decline. Give me the noisy and vibrant cacophony of Jamaica anytime.

So that was the horn explanation. Radar's occasional shout of "Make Chaos!" to passing vehicles will have to remain a mystery for now, like so much of this island.

I began to consider how well I had taken to this new climate and was very pleased with myself. I have begun moving like a grizzly bear in the mornings, padding slowly around and stretching out before ambling down to get breakfast and lolloping along at about half my normal speed for everything else. If you lived at the breakneck speed of the Western World here, you would die within a month such is the effect of the heat. Thus far I was burn free and still pasty white around the edges. A day at the beach would be a chance to address that. From a distance the beaches looked like rich people's playground with the obligatory sterile hulks of hotels along the front. Fortunately, we were not going to those beaches. As we descended the hill, we entered St Ann's Bay from where Marcus Garvey grew to become a hero of Black Nationalism. There is a school named after him here, and a mural of the great man is painted outside the entrance to the town that I vowed to visit again to pay homage to the great man.

As we crossed Church River, somewhat apt for a Sunday, the coast to my right was punctuated by bobbing boats and crystal-clear flashes of water. We took a right turn into Priory and were immediately assailed by Bob Marley's "Is this Love?" It seems that Bob is the staple for the coastal areas and touristy towns whereas it seems that he is not played so much on the radio these days. Still, it was like receiving a greeting from a welcoming friend. We parked up and I gained my first proper glimpse of the Caribbean Sea, and it did not disappoint. The sun was positively bouncing off the soft waves which glittered with every ebb and flow. The beach was busy with locals but not overcrowded and it was surrounded by a bay that ensured the soft winds were not a problem. As I moved onto the undulating sands, I took in my first close view of a Jamaican beach. The bar was doing a good trade as was the man offering horse rides through the shoreline. The fishing boats were not in use today and were instead parked up waiting for Monday morning's gruelling ritual. A bundle of Dreads was sheltering under the trees and grooving to the tunes being pumped out of the bar's loudspeakers. Another Dread was outside the distant toilet block making big shapes to the music of his prophet Bob. Further along the shore a group of young men were playing keepy-uppy with a football whilst everybody else was either peacefully floating along in the sea or reclined on the beach chatting loudly and animatedly to each other.

The sea was amazing. Unlike in British seaside resorts, where you get to that point on entering the water where the first wave brushes the underside of a bollock sending you thirty foot into the air, the walk into the Jamaican sea is like wading into a pleasantly warm bath. I have never known natural water to be so warm anywhere else, aside perhaps from the Dead Sea, my most unpleasant swimming experience. You might float, but it feels like you are floating in grease and God help you if you have any cuts. This was a most pleasing sea and like almost all other aspects of the island it was so relaxing. Having swum for a while, I found myself covetously looking at the now proceeding football match taking place on the sands. I wandered over and uttered a phrase I have not used since I was about twelve years old.

"Any game?" I asked.

"Sure man", came the reply and I was swiftly introduced to my team and pointed in the direction we were shooting. Now these boys are swift. Many of them looked like real athletes unlike my good self who looks like everything but a real athlete. Still, I held my own, and felt I gained some insight into the paucity of Jamaican appearances at the World Cup Finals. All the guys playing here either wanted to beat one man too many or wanted to exhibit football trickery much to the detriment of the team advancing up the pitch. I also failed to grasp one other of the major principles of the game. If the ball goes into the sea, you must get to it first to regain possession regardless of how far or deep it has gone. I was explained several rules in double quick time but didn't really grasp them. The Dread explaining them to me spoke so quickly and impenetrably that when he looked at me for confirmation that I had understood what he had said, all I could offer was a nod and a half-hearted and non-committal "Eeeeeeeeeeeee".

Now my playing style has developed over the years. I used to be a left winger, all trickery and ball crossing skills. When I was moved into centre midfield, my job was to disrupt the flow of the other team, tackle and then distribute the ball to get an attack moving. However, as my age has risen and my skills diminished, I am now a centre back and my mantra is "if in doubt, boot it out" referring to the ball and "if it moves, kick it" referring to the man. Consequently, my hoofs out of play into the Caribbean Sea should have been followed by a mad dash into the ocean to keep possession, but quite frankly, in this heat I was incapable. After about ten minutes I could have been mistaken for Moby Dick, I was blowing so hard. I said goodbye to my team-mates and limped off into the sea to cool down.

After a quick dip it seemd that Radar was anxious to get a move on so we all headed to the showers. These were cold water fountains and I have never enjoyed a cold shower quite so much. I could have stayed there for hours. A Dread stood by the showers collecting $20 JMD for the privilege (about 20 cents/15 pence). In between his collections, he was dancing like a loon. His friend then walked towards the showers, put his hand on the wooden fence at the back of them and proceeded to have a piss. I have noticed this a few times now. Some Jamaican men seem to piss anywhere. They piss on post boxes, house walls, the side of cars, anywhere. Pissy-pants then returned and did that Jamaican thing of barely moving to the sound, but just doing enough to show that he was indeed grooving.

As we left Priory beach, Jerk stalls were setting up for the Stone Love sound system gig that was playing on the beach later that night. The smells were delicious, but Radar was (not surprisingly given he was behind the wheel again) a man in a hurry. He wanted to get back to go and watch some local football/soccer matches, and I was invited along.

On our drive back up the steep and twisting roads Radar pointed out where Franklyn Rose, the West Indian batsman had grown up. Just opposite this village was coincidentally a group of cricketers dressed in all sorts of clothing, none of it white, and a cricket pitch the like of which I have never seen before. It was perched on the edge of the world so that all that could be viewed beyond the boundary was the ocean. Consequently, when any shot was put up into the air it looked like it may disappear into infinity, or beyond. We closed in on Pleasanton and the clouds above began to look ominous. When the sky is threatening in England I mumble and grumble at the prospect of rain. In Jamaica, I welcome it, because it never really interrupts the flow of the day unless it is torrential. As such I still had high hopes for the football match I was going to see.

Chapter Eight

Who Da Bumbaclaat in de Black?

After a quick and delicious Sunday dinner of roast chicken, rice and peas prepared by Momma (the vegetarian thing wasn't going well at all), I was whisked out of the house towards Claremont. Michael the mechanic who has known the family for a couple of years and who is a bit of a sportsman, was chauffer today and after Radar's speedway driving this morning, it was a welcome relief to be driving at a more relaxed and sedate pace.

I was trying to discover more about the upcoming match, but no-one seemed to know too much. I was told that it was eleven-a-side, six-a-side, half an hour, one hour, and ninety minutes long. No-one knew which teams were playing, but it was a local competition. I was pretty much in the dark. I did not know that this was to be one of my most memorable and funniest excursions so far. As we arrived at the ground, I was stunned. Cars lined the road, and there was approximately fifty or so vehicles in the field, very approximately parked up. To my left, in a hollow in the middle of the mountains was indeed a football pitch. What I had expected to be the equivalent of a Sunday League amateur game, it may still have been, was being attended by a considerable crowd of about 300 people.

But it was the riot of colour and movement that again exploded before my eyes. Kids were hanging off the crossbars, sitting on the crossbars, and using the crossbars as a kind of static zip line. The grandstand was full of people, in fact so full that there was a strip of spectators sat on the roof, legs dangling over the side. It looked like utter anarchy in practise. A car was pumping out the latest dancehall tunes for the whole ground, before, during and after the game. The smell of barbeque food was everywhere, and the hole in a wall that served as the bar was doing a roaring trade. Michael, Radar, Buzzy and I made our way to a suitable spot to watch from. This would normally consist of moving through the crowd uttering "Excuse me" as you weaved in and out. But this is not Buzzy style, as I was about to discover. Firstly, the route must be carefully selected in order that it includes as many pretty young girls as possible with as little space between them as possible. Buzzy then walked up to each of them, placed his hands all over their waist and sometimes their 'batties', and whispered "Scuse me baby..." into their ear.

Once Buzzy had sated his needs, we found a spot and got ready for the spectacle that was about to unfold. The kits looked like relics from the eighties and Norwich City's colours were prevalent. Footwear was variable, with some of the players wearing boots with the various stripes and flashes that suggest they cost a great deal, whilst others appeared to be wearing their work shoes. The pitch was designed for six a side and therefore the kids sprawling over the full-size crossbars were able to continue their exertions uninterrupted. The six-a-side goals on the other hand could be filled by just standing in them and as such were more like ice hockey nets. I imagined a low scoring game. The pitch was barely green and was rutted with sand, which meant that when a particularly quick movement occurred, the players disappeared briefly behind a blizzard of orange smoke. The players were about to kick off, so I naturally assumed that the sounds would be switched off.

How stupid am I? This is Jamaica. The tunes sizzled on throughout the game.

The crowd went ballistic as the game started and they continued to be as entertaining as what was happening on the pitch. This game was no friendly. These players kicked hell out of each other for half an hour, pausing only briefly to have a well-deserved drink, before returning to knock hell out of each other again. Once more, the Jamaican football-ing psyche was on show. Above all else, look good, be flash and hold onto the ball for as long as possible. This only encouraged the opposition in each case to try to violently scythe down their opponents all the more. As such there were a number of close misses, missed opportunities, and outrageous X-rated tackles on show. The officials were, let's say, lacking in professionalism. The referee tended to stay rooted to one spot, whistle poised, regardless of which part of the pitch the game was now being played in. If there was an incident, he immediately launched into a long-legged sprint to make his decision, which he could not possibly make with any conviction because for the most part he was standing at the opposite end of the pitch. His linesman, having had an early debate with the referee about the validity of a throw-in, a discussion that went on for some minutes, was hardly watching the game. He stood on the touchline, head down, swaying to the tunes being played and using his flag to monitor the bass beat, when he wasn't chatting to friends in the crowd.

There is another similarity to be made with ice hockey, other than the size of the goals. Every time there was a crunching tackle, a ball in the face, or even better a ball in the crown jewels, the crowd went absolutely and utterly mental. They all cheered and yelled, and the shouts of "bullet, bullet" that accompanies so many dancehall tunes could be heard bellowing out. There was a similar reaction when the players made mistakes such as ballooning the ball over the bar. Everyone laughed. It seemed to me that the spectators had come to watch but that the actual football on show was of minimal importance. Far more entertaining was to laugh out loud and ridicule the players' mistakes.

I was chatting to Michael, who is a Manchester United and West Indian cricket aficionado, and we shot the breeze whilst keeping half an eye on the game. Meanwhile the anarchic nature, both on the pitch and pitch-side, reached new heights as the local side scored. Immediately there was a pitch invasion and the participants ranged from gangling young kids to big boned, middle-aged women. The invasion took the form of running across the length of the field, dancing, jigging, and much waving of hands. It was hilarious. Joyous and with the tongue firmly lodged in the cheek. The player's goal celebrations meanwhile were carbon copies of some of those elaborate examples that the Premiership throws up weekly, the main difference being that these players were not hemmed in by the stands and as such many finished their celebration in a neighbouring field. The celebration and the invasion happened every time there was a goal.

After the third goal I became aware of someone running full pelt towards me. I managed a body swerve as he shot through the gap I had just made. It was one of the substitutes. He was being chased by the referee who was trying to sprint and produce a card at the same time. The referee had obviously hoped to book him for encroaching onto the field of play, but this player, who had done a little more than 'encroach' by legging it across the width of the pitch, had disappeared behind me and so the referee gave up his chase and returned to the game.

By now, the night was beginning to make its presence felt, and the crowd were demanding that the floodlights be turned on, even though there were none. The whole spectacle was bright, fun, exciting, and it was so Jamaica.

The football match sums up the island for me. Rules seem to be in place in the country, but it appears that the people bend them as far as possible, simply in the name of having a good time.

The full-time whistle blew and so we made our way back to the car. Buzzy meanwhile sensed an opportunity and so any time he was behind a girl of any shape or size he was busy whispering "sssssssss...sexy!" in the hope of pulling even as darkness fell.

As one might guess, even leaving the game was a frenzied mess. The road which was next to the pitch was practically a single lane, so as Michael tried to negotiate all the cars and people and do a three-point turn, there was a lot of angry shouting and criticism, until one particular observer yelled "Go, do your thing, driver" and everyone stopped to allow Michael to complete his manoeuvre.

I think the boys were in a rush to get elsewhere after the game, but they of course had to drop me off first. As a result, Michael illustrated how he too had been to the Radar School of Driving, by remaining inches from the back of the car in front for the whole journey, before overtaking, you guessed it, on a corner.

The heavy dusk that hits Jamaica at about 7.30 in the evening had descended by now and yet still the roads were spotted with the dull shapes of people making their way along the road. I noticed several women walking alone and asked Radar whether this was a safe practice. He explained that incidents of rape and assault are very rare in this part of Jamaica. He went on to give the reason for this,

"Jamaica is a small place, and everybody know everybody. So, if something bad happen, someone, somewhere will find out who did it".

It seems that the deterrent to certain crimes in certain parts of Jamaica is mob rule, but one cannot argue with that too much when the crimes are of such seriousness. Buzzy then gave me his own inimitable take on things.

"This is why you have to be careful with the gals too, Isaac. You might chat up a gal and it might turn out that she knows someone who knows your girlfriend, and then you are in trouble!"

Radar explained that one time he had gone to meet his girlfriend, only to find his girlfriend and his gyal set next to each other at the bar. As if to illustrate this point, right on cue, we dropped off Buzzy where his girlfriend was waiting at the side of the road for him. It appeared like he might have some explaining to do judging by her 'screwface'.

When we reached home Jonesy was sitting on the step.

"Isaac, man, you didn't come to watch me playing cricket" he implored. I didn't even know he had been playing.

"I played good too, made a good score, forty."

I promised Jonesy I would try to catch him playing before my time here was out.

However, of more pressing concern was that my front and my back were lobster red following my beach exertions, and my confidence of coping with the climate was shattered now that I had removed my top. I looked like an overdone little red devil; I was just missing the trident and horns. Today had been a day of pure fun but I was about to pay for it with a painful sleep.

Chapter Nine

Fight, Fight, Fight!

As you might have gauged already, on the porch is where a great number of discussions take place in Jamaica. The discussion this morning was cars. Pops had taken his to be fixed because the brakes and tyres seemed worn. It was the car that we had done most of our travelling in so it wasn't too hard to work out why this might be the case, nor who was mainly responsible.

Whilst sitting there on another glorious morning I was mesmerised by the stunning noise of the insects. Poochie brought me out an unusual breakfast of chicken and fried dumplings and as I sat around listening to Momma and Pops chatting, I noticed that the noise of the insects was now threatening to drown Momma out. Then the sound dropped to a barely perceptible level, and then once more increased in a wave of noise. It was as if someone was hiding in the Gully and was operating the volume control from there. I tried to figure out if the noise increased or decreased with the sun moving out or moving into the clouds, but there was no discernible pattern. In the end I just put it down to another wonder of Jamaica.

I needed to get into Ocho Rios to change some money, but I had no idea how I might get there with Pop's car off the road. I suggested I get a taxi. The distance from Pleasanton to Ochi is approximately twenty kilometres. The cost of the taxi would be approximately $178 JA, about $1.30 US and about £1 in British money. I considered this a good deal, until Momma warned me of the pitfalls. Firstly, the taxi drivers make Radar look like *Driving Miss Daisy*. Taxi drivers in Jamaica are apparently the scourge of the roads because it is in their

Dazzling Ochi.

interest to get from A to B and back to A again in double quick time from a purely commercial point of view. In their quest to do this, they take no prisoners. Secondly, you share the taxi. Hence, you could be sharing your taxi with a farmer, a family, or the maniacal boyfriend of the local stylist. Interrupting the conversation someone shouted that Jonesy was coming up the road.

"He alive?" asked Momma.

We had a chat as Momma set about a one-woman cull of the mosquito population, pausing only to show Kaddy where the bodies were located on the floor.

"There is that likkle piece of ting" she would point as Kaddy dipped to pick them up. Kaddy's mom, DeeDee, phoned from Montego Bay to sort out the arrangements for my Sumfest related stay there. She then asked to speak to me and said that Kaydee was missing me.

It's the 'likkle' tings.

Meanwhile, a furious debate was taking place in the kitchen. Snoop, who knows England, was suggesting that English women were better looking than Jamaican women whilst Jonesy and Jay were being rightly patriotic. I was asked my opinion and tried to fudge the issue by talking about population ratios and the like.

It was looking like Ocho Rios was off the map for the day, so I decided to brave the walk into town. I was halfway down the main road when Michael appeared, and what was even better was that Michael appeared in a car. It emerged that he needed to go to Ochi to pick up his daughter from summer school, so he was more than happy to give me a lift. My opening gamut in the conversation was about the driving of Buzzy and Radar, which, in truth, once I had arrived safely at my destination and could look back retrospectively, I found to be exhilarating and exciting but others in the family found it to be terrifying.

Michael explained it thus: "When dem get behind the wheel, dem blood get hot!"

My eyes were fixed on the roadsides as we moved through the roads at a relatively calm pace. This was the road I had travelled on most often in Jamaica, and as such it was becoming a little more familiar but still, I scanned it for signs of new interest. It never fails to throw something up.

Today, I began to ruminate on particulars of the Jamaican make up. The way people walk has been discussed, as has the way people hang around, but today I saw a boy who epitomised the latter. He was draped over some wooden bars, limbs hanging loosely over the horizontal struts, surveying the passing world, dispassionately, like a lion. As the manner of walking on most Jamaicans has a unique way, so does the way people hang around. It is like an art form. There is no semblance of impatience or rushing; as if those hanging have believed it when someone told them; "Mi soon come".

Michael, it soon materialised, is the man with the connections on the island. Everyone seems to know him. He played cricket to a good standard even representing St Ann and as such gained a degree of local fame. He was talking about interviews he could set up for me which I felt was a step forward because I was conscious of the fact that my original reason for being here was floating by and that I had yet to cross swords or words with any of the people I had hoped to.

Michael had already been in touch with a friend of my absolute favourite artist, Sizzla, but one of the superstars of Jamaican reggae was "not on the island" so a hoped-for trip to Judgement Yard would not be happening on this trip. As an aside, Sizzla's 2020 Covid Sumfest appearance is well worth a watch since it is indeed sizzling in righteousness and star quality.

Michael further suggested that the island's reggae radio station, Irie F.M. was in Ocho Rios and that we could pass by to see if anyone was about. But before that we had to make the descent once more through my old friend, the 3km Fern Gully. According to Michael, the Gully road follows the route of a river and as such it occasionally floods. Last year a car was trapped in the Gully for three hours and Michael stopped by at a shack en-route to try to catch a friend who had gained local fame in saving seven people when another flood had threatened to drown them. Unfortunately, he was not in. A theme was beginning to take hold. So instead, whilst we were driving, I was shown the caves that litter the route and some of the hidden paths that take locals to their homes above the Gully. Suddenly and as if by magic a long rangy Rasta appeared. He was grey of dread, and his beard was a magnificent construction. He was barefoot and had on a pair of jeans that threatened to fall apart but for the moment clung to his body in rebellion. An off-white string vest covered his upper-half, and he was making his way down the Gully with the aid of a huge stick. After we had passed him, I looked back but he had majestically and magically disappeared. Jah moves in mysterious ways.

As we entered the town once more, the schools were emptying and Ocho Rios Primary School was a vast dash of vividness and movement. On the main wall of the school was a mural of all of Jamaica's National Symbols and Heroes, with Marcus

Mosiah Garvey dominant in the middle. These same pictures adorn the covers of children's exercise books, a constant reminder of the struggle Jamaica has undertaken to get where she is today.

Michael drove me to where I had changed money previously, and one of the attempted heroes of the Poochie shoe drama was sat there. Michael knew him and so both Michael and I exchanged fist bumps with the man. The man had initially tried to get me into his shop but the fact I was with Michael made it clear that I was not a souvenir seeker for now.

Michael introduced me to him; it was West Indian cricketer Franklyn Rose's brother. After some small talk, we moved onto the Western Union building and exchanged my money.

The route back began with a fill up at the Esso Petrol Station. This normally mundane procedure was transformed into a mini drama, because, this might well be an Esso petrol station, but it is a Jamaican Esso petrol station. As we drove into it, cars were criss-crossing each other in bizarre random directions. Similarly, the pedestrians moved according to no law of nature, stepping out in front of vehicles, running, jogging, dancing, or of course, just hanging around. The forecourt was absolutely teeming with people and vehicles. It doesn't help that several of the latter seem to use the petrol station as a short cut to avoid the traffic lights that are situated next to it. Once more everyone is loud, horns are constantly blasted, and the petrol station is a spattering of colour, sound, and vibe.

Michael had gone into the kiosk to buy some bits as I observed one particular group of men, numbering about twenty, becoming vexed sounding as they surrounded two minibuses. The vexation hit a crescendo, and if fists didn't fly, they almost did. There was certainly plenty of scuffling, raised arms, pushing and shoving, with t-shirts and tank tops twisting and twirling. Amid all this were some locals, one of whom was a woman carrying a young girl. Eventually three of the men surrounded the local woman with the girl and bundled her into the minibus despite a few other men trying to prevent her getting in. It was reminiscent of the tales you hear of those who have returned from a Middle East kidnapping. When Michael returned, he explained that they were two competing taxi minibus services fighting (almost literally) for trade. Momma was right about taxis then and having initially been excited at the thought of travelling with the locals, I now considered giving the experience a wide berth.

Many of those on the forecourt were sucking on bags. These contain various frozen juices and are called, somewhat predictably, Bag Juice. We picked up a couple of bags and moved back towards Pleasanton, picking up Michael's daughter on the way. The school was a nondescript building, but the sound of a male schoolteacher bellowing through the open window was universally familiar.

On the route home we moved through Walkers Wood, and I wondered which of the ladies clamped to the back of the motorcycles that passed through Pleasanton a few evenings ago had sashayed away with the honour of the title Miss Walkers Wood. Walkers Wood incidentally, is one of the areas where peppers and seasoning is produced before its transference to island wide stores and a number of Afro-Caribbean stores worldwide.

We also passed a building construction site which was in the process of creating an army camp. Michael once more explained that the previous army base in Newcastle was too cold (and this was Newcastle, Jamaica - I cannot imagine how

That walk!

they would have coped in Newcastle, England), hence the need to build one in a warmer environment.

Michael then took me to his place of work which is a garage in the middle of the town. Here stand shells of Japanese automobiles that Michael buys over the internet and then makes roadworthy again before selling them on. Inside his office he has a computer set up to make his purchases and he kindly allowed me to check my e-mail. I had been invited to a press conference on Friday where some of the biggest Sumfest artistes will be. I now felt comfortable in town again and was no longer looking over my shoulder for MACHETEMAN, maybe as a result of me cutting down my weed consumption which might still be referred to as 'prodigious'.

When I got home Jonesy was asleep on the porch. He was reclined over a chair like a giant, friendly bear. Every time he appeared to be waking up, he just shifted position and went back to sleep. I am not too surprised that Jonesy likes his sleep. He is a coffee bean farmer up in the Blue Mountains which I imagine to be strenuous labour. Buzzy sat on the sidewalk on the other side of the street, chatting to, you guessed it, a young woman, whilst Radar was cleaning the car. I had a brief chat with Momma and Pops, and then after a drink and one of Pop's conical masterpieces, I hit the hay for a siesta only to be awoken at 9pm by the arrival of Michael who wanted to take me to Faith's Pen.

Faith's Pen is one of the Jerk centres of Jamaica. A row of about thirty little shacks huddle next to each other on one of the island's major routes. The fare they sell is exotic (and expensive), including meats such as fish, chicken, and pork, all liberally sprinkled with Jerk seasoning as well as the compliments to the meat such as bammies, festival dumplings and breadfruit. The locals cruise up and down the strip upon which these shacks stand before choosing their vendor and parking up. Opposite the shacks are little alcoves for eaters to sit down and take their time over this delicious food. Given the limited options for vegetarians I am afraid to say I once more succumbed to the chicken. Tomorrow, I decided, I would return to my vegetarian ways. My vegetarianism would "soon come".

On the way back we stopped off at a bar. This involved the unusual process of Michael banging on the grille until someone woke up to come and serve us. Then the giant gates were unlocked by the sleepy headed soul, and we were shown inside. We were later joined by a bus driver called Phil, who it had to be hoped, was not behind the wheel that evening. He entertained us with his pub tricks involving straws and his outrageous factual knowledge, all of which was blatantly untrue. By this time, I was on my last legs having only had two Red Stripe beers, so we bade our farewells and headed home. It seems that Jamaica is a land bounteous with many things, but what it has above all, is real character. The people make the place and at times they can be polite, funny, and cheerful whilst at others angry, aggressive and violent. One thing is certain. Jamaica is far from dull.

Chapter Ten

The Road to Sumfest

This was it; the first of four days that I fully expected to leave me exhausted, drained and in need of heavy stimulation. Ever since I arrived on the island the expectation and excitement for THE event of the year has been cranking up. Every day it is advertised in newspapers, announced on the radio and plugged on the TV. It is BIG, and I was beginning to feel a little bit out of my depth. Today entailed a trip to Mo' Bay to pick up the passes for Sumfest before returning to Pleasonton for our final sleep before the chaos of the 'Greatest Reggae Show on Earth'. Each day there have been headlines relating to Sumfest in *The Star* newspaper; most notably relating to Beenie Man, Ninja Man and Mavado being banned from most of the big hotels in Montego Bay. It seems there have been problems in the past relating to sizes of entourage, behaviour, rae rae! I began my journey in Jamaica with the *Daily Gleaner* newspaper as a guide but soon realised that *The Star* is perhaps closer to the heart of Jamaica in that it has a sense of fun and ridiculousness and some of its reporting is linguistically quaint, and so I was now reading both to get a real feel for Jamaica and its daily concerns, which *The Star* has a habit of sensationalising with screaming headlines. For instance, in the same edition that had the hotel story on the front page there were two further headlines that said a lot about the country. *Man Jailed for Stealing Goats* is an illustration that Jamaica is predominantly a rural community aside from the big cities whilst the second bellowed *Couple Accused of Assault and Obeah*. Obeah is the practice of dark magic that still holds sway over a portion of the island, and regardless of whether you are a believer or think it is all mumbo jumbo, many in Jamaica take it very seriously indeed. The following day's copy headlined a story about a community disturbed by constant partying under the title *Noisy Gay Men Evicted*. The story continued,

"A group of boisterous homosexuals who had been disturbing the community of Chevy Chase in Havendale, St Andrew were evicted on Monday..."

Two things are notable here; one being the use of the word 'boisterous' which seems to hark back to a bygone age where stereotypes of homosexuality focused on camp and outrageous behaviour , and the other is that there is actually a place called Chevy Chase. However, the article also hints at one of the island's darker aspects, its still prevalant homophobia. Given that dancehall music is one of the avenues for free expression in Jamaica, I am prepared for similar, possibly more blatant expressions at Sumfest.

Before I left the house, a lottery had taken place. I had two passes booked for the event and could therefore take A.N.Other to the show as my P.A.. Poochie won and as such she became chief photographer. I had two cameras with me, only one of which worked, but I suggested she take both to make us "look professional".

Fat chance.

As I left the safe environs of my Pleasanton home I overheard a conversation between Momma and a friend taking place outside. The latter had seen my gift of a red, gold and green vest on the washing line but not me, and had asked if Momma's guest was Ras(ta).

"Yes" said Momma. "He a baldhead Rastafari!"

A weaker man might begin to get a complex.

We were taking two journeys today, the first leg with Momma and Pops, the second with Ras Kelvin. Momma had put some heavy stuff in the boot for Pops to drop off on his return journey so the first debate of the day was on which side to position ourselves on to even the weight out, purely for the well-being of the vehicle. Once we were moving, I began my daily observation. Two doors down from where I was living was a house with an enormous weed plant just growing there. I mulled over the fact that no-one had taken it, but I guess that it is in such plentiful supply that no-one needs to. As we moved out of Pleasanton, I noticed a man walking with something brightly coloured in his hand. He was stocky of build, serious of demeanour, had huge work boots on, and the brights colours belonged to the chicken he was holding upside down as he marched determinedly to wherever it was he was heading. He almost made my 'character of the day', but further into the journey I came across two more worthy contenders. A man in his later twenties sat astride a cool looking motorbike. He was trimmed of head and beard and was wearing the darkest of shades topped off with a black beret. On his top half he wore a button-down v neck t-shirt, black and white in pattern and held in place by a pair of white braces. His trousers were black, but crucially, ended by his ankles in order that his matching socks were on view. His shoes were slick and shiny. He was coolness personified. However, he was beaten into second place by a man on a pedal bike. Since I have been in Jamaica I have seen people carrying all sorts of objects on their heads, from buckets to boxes to bag juice and I have been amazed at the balance and dexterity of the carriers but today's bike rider will take some surpassing. He was sashaying along the road on his bicycle whilst balancing a bottle of wine on his head. This was not some fancy circus performer nor was it being done for tourists; this guy was simply going about his day. Jamaica constantly astonishes me with its lovely lunacy.

My 'sign of the day' is one I have started to see in several places. It simply orders "NO IDLERS". This tickled me because it suggests that there are idlers. Who are these people? What do they do? Idle? Are they the ones I see just 'hanging around'? Meanwhile, above the haunts of the idlers, hundreds of John Crow were stalking the skies. When their shadow crosses the bonnet of the car, it is a chilling site. It's in their pace too. The way they circle is deathly ominous. Jamaica is a country of layers and layers of land. Some of the scenery is like one of those children's pop-up books, and people's gardens are blizzards of symmetry offset with touches of randomness. The colours of the flag are in the land; black, gold, and green. The people are amazing to look at too, not just regarding their fashion sense but also in their gorgeous smiles and in their occasional sullen look, a common feature of the girls that you see working the stalls on the roadside who look like they are seriously not to be messed with. Humour is never far away though. A man had pulled up in his car to 'relieve' himself and his 'pal' had kindly taken it upon himself to stand on the opposite side of the road and laughingly point and bellow to the passing cars that all had their windows down,

"Look 'pon what that boy is doing over der!"

On our journey today we witnessed further examples of the nature of the taxi drivers which again served to warn me of going anywhere near them. One overtook Pops, realised he was passing his destination and cut in front of Pops, slammed on the brakes, and parked, whilst Pops swerved to avoid paying a cab fare.

As we hit a town called Salem it became apparent that we were cruising into commercialism. This was confirmed by a sign marked *Hedonism III* which is one of the no-holds barred sex resorts so beloved of British and American tourists. Just beyond this point was where the 'switch' occurred so Poochie and I bade farewell to Momma and Pops, and stepped into Ras Kelvin's familiar vehicle. We drove into Montego Bay on the flat coastal road. Aside from the shacks and the sea, there is little of interest on these more industrialised routes.

Once we had arrived in Montego Bay, my first task was to try to get myself straight having been fed the 'erb by both Pops and Kelvin all morning and to get into the Hotel that would serve as headquarters for the production team to pick up our media passes. I am not a great fan of grand hotels because whenever I am in them I don't feel like I should be there. When the doorman opened the hotel's gleaming glass entrance for me, I felt that he could sense my unease. I nervously paced through the hallway and found the entrance to the temporary HQ. As Kelvin, Poochie and I walked through to the Sumfest suite the scale of the operation became apparent. People were permanently and noisily manning computers and telephones, whilst an array of immaculately dressed Sumfest organisers dished out passes and brochures. I picked up our passes and chatted briefly with Marcia who had been responsible for ensuring I was successful in my application and to a couple of other members of the smiling and welcoming team. The atmosphere was slick, professional, and above all, friendly. Sumfest is being billed as the Biggest Reggae Show on Earth and given the list and calibre of artists that are performing it would be difficult to argue with that tag. All the people sat in the Sumfest media room looked happy but braced for an incredibly busy and long weekend.

Our first stop on the way back was via one of Ras Kelvin's 'bredren'. Living on the beach in an idyllic little shack which is also a type of convenience store, my new acquaintance was a diminutive Rasta, quite possibly in his fifties, who put me to shame with his six-pack and physique.

Kelvin placed a $100 JMD on the counter and asked for a "bush of weed". His friend disappeared into the back and returned with something approaching the street value of £100/$130US in the holy herb. It was chopped up and placed in a spliff with no tobacco, and then passed to me. It is what is known as an 'ital' spliff. As previously mentioned, ital refers to food but also tobacco as well as several other products, and it basically means that something is pure and without additives. This particular ital wonderment tasted of mint and kept me quietly dazed for about two hours. We then moved on to a guest house that Kelvin had arranged for us to stay in for the duration of the Sumfest. It was $14,000 JA for three nights, the price some hotels in Montego Bay were charging for one night. It was a little too close to Rose Hall for me, where legend has it the ghost of a woman who murdered her husband patrols the grounds. Security was not as high as I had hoped for either but given that the Sumfest begins at 7.00 p.m. every evening and finishes at 6.00 a.m. every morning, the likelihood was that I would be sleeping in the day so I figured it would be ok. This was to be our base from tomorrow.

Ras Kelvin's house is a small distance from the guesthouse, so we popped in to visit the family on our way back. Kelvin and DeeDee live in a cosy and colourful house within 400 yards of the sea. The area in which their home is set is composed of a cluster of small abodes packed randomly around each other and surrounded by the most idyllic of sites. The hamlet begins where the mountains end, and ends where the sea begins. Children play without cares on the street as Kelvin's mother, a statuesque lady, watches with indolent interest. She was sat outside next to her husband's grave. It seems to me that burying your relatives in your garden or backyard is extremely humane and as mentioned earlier, I can think of nothing better than being able to sit and share life with the person you really miss but still love every single day.

When we returned to Pleasanton, Buzzy was frying some fish outside known as 'Errin' Spratt. Everyone was gathered at the back or down the sides of the house either chatting, thinking, singing, or simply resting. I was getting a drink of juice when I heard an almighty commotion outside which involved shouting, banging and laughter. Apparently, Jonesy had swallowed one of his false teeth causing him to choke and so the banging noise was Radar slapping Jonesy's back to try to dislodge the errant tooth and fortunately he was successful. The laughter was Buzzy's of course.

As everyone sat and chatted, Ras Kelvin retained a slight distance between himself and the rest of the group. He appeared to be deep in thought until the conversation got around to music. There was talk of Bob Marley and Nine Mile, and Kelvin began to philosophise about Bob. He suggested that when people hear a tune on the radio, they identify it as Bob Marley. However, the tune is more likely than not by Bob Marley *AND* the Wailers. Kelvin believes that Bunny Wailer and Peter Tosh have become forgotten men in the Bob story, and yet both have produced their own music that is stunning in its own right, especially Peter who was the real rebel Wailer, frequently taking on the police and taking on the authorities and Babylon shitstem whilst taking no shit. In both his lyrics and interviews he is stridently BLACK and PROUD and his commitment to railing against the injustices of the prevailing racism of the wider world was both breath-taking and wildly admirable. If you hadn't guessed it, Kelvin's view is one I share.

Bunny and Peter's contribution to Bob's music is perhaps best encapsulated in the BBC's *Old Grey Whistle Test* performance of The Wailers' *Concrete Jungle*. It is the high watermark of Bob Marley's career. Bunny and Peter's backing vocals along with their consummate playing, lifts that wonderful song to a completely different level and place altogether. Even now, a full fifty years later, it makes for a remarkable and riveting watch and listen. At that time, The Wailers were at their sartorial coolest and musically hottest and tightest, and in my humble opinion was never matched in the seven years that remained of Bob Marley's life. The loss of Bob and Peter was the loss of two amazing talents and now that Bunny has joined them they will likely be pleasing Jah with their mystical ways. Whilst he was alive he continued performing and still talked the most sense of most of the artists I have heard on the island. In the documentary *Made in Jamaica*, Bunny's comment are incisive, poetic, and cannot be argued with. The man talks sense in the same way that Bob did but because of Bob's early and tragic death both Bunny and Peter's words are sometimes drowned out by the echo of Robert Nesta Marley's own wise utterances, which continue to drift down the years. Kelvin's take on Marley is that he was a great man but that is not to say a greater man might not be working his way up now.

Seeing Radar and Kelvin sat next to each other was an interesting juxtaposition. It was like witnessing a standoff between the secular and the spiritual. Radar, short and stocky, was sat on a step wearing jeans, white vest top and a big bling-bling silver cross across his chest and as one expects with Radar, he was performing snippets of songs that are current hits on the radio. Meanwhile Kelvin, long and rangy, wore jeans and a gold, and green vest. Around his neck was a silver 'erb leaf and his shoulders were draped in a patterned shirt, upon which were two pin badges exalting H.I.M Hailie Selassie.

There is room for both in Jamaica.

In the evening Kelvin and I reasoned on the porch for three long hours about music, the Rasta faith and Jamaica in general. Our chat was interrupted only by Kelvin bursting into song, every one of them having a depth and emotional Ras intelligence about it. This is partly what I came to Jamaica to see; Jah in action through one of the adherents of the Rastafari faith. This was rootsy Rastafari and it seemed to be a suitable pre-cursor to tomorrow when I will be exposed to some of the more commercial aspects of the faith at the self-proclaimed Greatest Reggae Show on Earth.

Chapter Eleven

The Greatest Reggae Show on Earth

Overnight rain had given Jamaica a much-needed break from the sweltering heat, and it meant that the island would be refreshed for the opening of the behemoth that is Reggae Sumfest.

The drive down to Montego Bay was an exciting one but I was conscious of the fact that many of the locals I passed on the journey would not be able to afford the (by our standards) relatively cheap tickets. As we drove this morning with the obligatory pounding reggae soundtrack it felt like being in a film; the scenery, people going about their work, noise, shouts, and laughter, all added a sense of vibrancy to this mini epic.

When I made eye contact with passers-by it was noticeable that many quickly and somewhat bashfully averted their gaze as if I was loaded up with a television camera behind me aimed directly at them. It betrays humility and shyness. Meanwhile the drive has become like going to the National Gallery every day, and I am beginning to remember where each of my favourite 'works of art' is stationed on the road. Ras Kelvin's van is fitted with enormous speakers so that the sounds boom out on every journey we take. Consequently, I am beginning to become familiar with some of the decade old tunes by some of the stars that will be at Sumfest. They are given heavy rotation on the radio; Morgan Heritage's *Nothing to Smile About*, Lutan Fyah's *Africa*, Richie *Spice's The World is a Cycle* and *Di Plane Land*, and Etana's *I Am Not Afraid*. Jamaicans listen to music differently to audiences in the US and UK. For instance, if I hear a song I like by an artist at home I am likely to go out and buy their album. In Jamaica, the people just love the song. They are often not too fussed with who sings a song they like, because as a rule Jamaicans tend to listen to mix tapes and as such the song is just one of many by several different artists. So, my insistence on knowing "Who is that singing?" often went unanswered.

Today I discovered a new addition to the car horn code. Kelvin beeps to any fellow Rasta he spots, and we seem to encounter several of them across the length and breadth of the island. Kelvin also demonstrated that the hard shoulder serves a different function on Jamaican roads. It is used to avoid oncoming, overtaking traffic. The number of close shaves we have on this drive alone has been considerable. As we reached sea level, my ears popped, clearing them for the assault they were set to receive tonight. The roads were littered with Babylon, as the police were pulling vans over and checking them as they entered Montego Bay. Kelvin explained that they were checking to make sure that "Everyone go in clean". He explained this as he pulled on his latest big fat joint. I had seen Kelvin overtake a police car earlier on the journey and in celebration of his manoeuvre he exhaled a huge plume of ganja smoke out of the window.The traffic was heavy which was good, because it meant that Kelvin had to slow down a little. My Rasta friend had moved rapidly into pole position with Radar as joint scariest driver.

The crawl into the Sumfest compound was tortuous. Cars came in at all angles competing for the single lane that took you through the gates. Once inside there was a police patrol situated to the left, and given that Kelvin is a Rasta, I figured that we were likely to get pulled over. Sure enough, we were. I was a little concerned because I remembered slipping a joint into my shorts pocket earlier in the day and was unsure whether I had smoked it or not. Therein lies the problem with the 'erb; short term memory loss.

As I got out of the van cloaked in a smell that must have made the armed police officers suddenly feel hungry, I was asked; "Do you have any firearms?" "Huh?"

"Do you have any firearms?" he repeated.

"Me? Er no", I replied, remembering that I had left my sub-machine gun back in Pleasanton.

It must have been blatantly obvious that I was high, but I was defiantly high and in such a condition that I wanted to leave the cop with the suspicion that maybe I might just be the kind of person to own something like a vicious assault rifle, especially now that I knew that this was not a drugs search. But then it became one. I had a full pat down, everything on my person was checked, even my cigarette packet, and I had a full-on scan with one of their electronic detectors. Then he went through the pat down again obviously unable to believe that a white member of the press (ahem) would turn up at the Biggest Reggae Show on Earth without a spliff or two. He headed down to my pockets and I don't know if he sensed my body stiffen or not but he seemed to take an age rummaging through them. All the time I was wondering how Kelvin was getting on around the other side of the van because I could not believe that he would be travelling without his holy herb. They searched the van and then told us we were free to leave. As we moved towards the entrance, Kevin pulled on what remained of a spliff. He had had it cupped in his hand throughout the duration of the search. I felt inside my pocket to find it empty. Lucky.

Poochie and I bade farewell to Kelvin at the gate and made our way towards the media tent; she laden with cameras and me laden with trepidation. Inside the venue it was empty. We

Anthony B

were way too early. We had been told to arrive at 7p.m. which we had duly done only to be confronted with an empty tent. We decided to go and tour the venue and discovered that our passes gave us prime access to the front of the stage and the VIP section. We spotted Kelvin by the back of the VIP area/front of the public viewing section and went over for a chat through the fence. Kelvin had had to leave us and return to the main entrance to enter the venue. There he was searched, and a pocketknife and some weed were found. The knife was confiscated, but the weed was given back. Looks like tomorrow night I can return to my merry smoking ways then, and that my panic during the search was unwarranted. After conversing with Kelvin for a few minutes, I became aware of a moving presence behind the fence down towards my left-hand side. I looked hard and saw a couple on a pair of stools, chatting whilst scowling up at me. I looked harder still, and a flash of recognition swept across me, it was FAT FOOTBALL HEAD!

He had obviously recognised me so I did the gracious thing and with my being in the VIP area milked it for all it was worth. I spun and twirled my VIP pass around trying to look important, played exaggeratedly with my green press band and casually leant on the fence, the one the separated me, a VIP, from FAT FOOTBALL HEAD, a bog-standard punter. It was lucky there was a fence separating us judging by the murderous look in his eyes. Kelvin must have wondered what had got into me.

Eventually the media trickled through in all their brash and self-important glory. I felt real sympathy for the staff at Sumfest who must have to deal with many of these seemingly arrogant and self-important ego-laden souls. However, at the start of the festival, everyone was bright of mind and of appearance. When the lovely people from Touchstone Productions arrived I gave them names of those we would like to interview. Top of my list was Anthony B because I have been a fan of his for some time and felt he could best appraise aspects of Jamaican/Rastafari culture that I was most interested in because he is one the recognised kings of conscious dancehall. I listed further artists but given the presence of MTV and other such big names I felt the chance of little ol' me meeting the big, big stars was going to be somewhat limited.

And then it was showtime.

Chapter Twelve

Here I Am Now, Entertain Me

Dancehall music is synonymous with homophobia. I despise homophobia and racism equally, but I believe the homophobia that is attached to this genre is tongue in cheek and is simply a way for artists to play up to the crowd. This doesn't mean I excuse it, nor that I think it's harmless because I also understand that in Jamaica it can have serious repercussions for those identified as gay. There must be ways to tackle it here and it can only be hoped that it will soon disappear on the island as elsewhere. Personally, I choose to challenge it head on but I know that others suggest that in appearing to be bothered by it only heightens its effect and that we should just let it go over our heads and as a result artists who consider homophobia as a means to gain notoriety and fame would soon realise that there is not much capital to be made out of it and turn it in. When I was growing up in the UK, homophobia, like racism was still rife but it seems to have dissipated as we have become more tolerant as a society. Sadly racism is still a feature in that newly Brexited island. I was aware that I was more than likely going to come face to face with lyrics of a violent and homophobic nature on Dancehall Night, but I was determined for one night only to turn my mind off to that and just focus on being entertained otherwise this potentially one-off opportunity for me would likely be ruined. As a result of closing my mind to it for one night, the show left me utterly shell-shocked.

Dancehall Night was quite simply the most fantastic spectacle I have witnessed and the headlines were made on the first night of the whole weekend. The Beenie Man vs Bounty Killer 'beef' that has variously festered or exploded over the years finally reached its apogee. Tonight, one of them went too far and it ensured that Bounty's evening/morning ended with a scuffle with the police before being escorted from the premises. However, it was not for that reason that Dancehall Night was a night to remember for me, because as with so many things on the island, the people made the occasion. A magnificent line up was complimented by a crowd dressed to impress, and wishing to be entertained. Dancehall is exactly the right genre to ensure the crowd would get their money's worth. One of the greatest things about Reggae Sumfest is the sheer effort everybody makes. From the organisers down to the punters, everything is done to ensure that Sumfest is an occasion filled with colour, laughter, fun and vitality.

Waiting for the entrance of each artist is heightened by the fact that you never know what on earth they might look like. Jamaican dancehall artists are renowned for having the most extravagant dress sense and tonight did not disappoint. Conversely the crowd, especially the females, seem to make an effort to undress and expose every single inch of flesh whilst just not crossing into the boundaries of indecent exposure.

The daunting task of opening Sumfest was gifted to Nature, an artist who was on former English Premiership Footballer Ricardo Gardener's record label and whose music is inspiring in a rootsy culture way. Nature's opening quiet demeanour and Rasta consciousness was contrasted with act number two, the on-rushing Shane-O wearing an outfit straight out of Warner Brothers. In fact, it is the case that nearly every artist here tonight has something of the cartoon about him or her, either in dress, image, or reputation. Alley Cat wore a white suit topped off with an accompanying fedora, whilst Madd Dogg administered the first injection of sexual humour with his four female dancers who were mostly on the large side and not the most dextrous.

In some respects Dancehall is not too far removed from Benny Hill or Carry On, just a little more X rated, and the crowd lap it up. I have never been to a gig before where there are frequent bouts of raucous laughter, and it is very much the case that the artists here play up to this. The quality remained high throughout as Busy Signal, I Octane, Konshens, Bugle, Serani, Harry Toddler, Vybz Kartel, D.I., Assassin and Erup all delivered sets of real vitality and talent. There were no band changes initially, as a house band performed for most of the artistes, so save for the odd ten-minute break in order for the crowd to recuperate, the music flowed constantly for around five hours. When the headliners did require changes, they were slick and quick, and there was none of the interminable waiting that you get at English festivals. Most of these artists are by now well established and it appears that the future of dancehall remains secure in their hands. However as with any festival, there are always defining highlights.

The first outstanding performance of the night was by Munga Honourable, who delivered a rat-a-tat set of quick-fire delivery and Rasta passion which he claims makes him the instigator of 'Gangster-Ras'. He was quickly followed by two of the island's finest females, Macka Diamond and D' Angel, who threw in sets of high energy and glamour, both having chosen outrageous outfits for the show. Macka entered to a shower of money with her visage printed on the notes and wore a gold jumpsuit with a low cleavage (naturally) whilst the ex-Mrs Beenie Man, D'Angel, morphed from her chosen moniker into a PVC-clad vamp. My fellow St. Ann resident Little Hero was a popular act and some of the songs he aired from his past sounded mightily impressive.

And then came the moment I had been waiting for. Enter Anthony B. The righteous passion was absent tonight as he decided to go with a more dancehall orientated set and he had the crowd in hysterics with some of his antics, most notably when he stood arms folded at centre stage, defiance plastered across his face whilst former Prime Minister Bruce Golding's comments on an interview from BBC Hard Talk were played to the crowd. In the interview, Golding had said that homosexuals might well become members of the Government, but "Not in my Cabinet". Anthony B's stance said it all; It is not me saying this, it's the former Prime Minister. And so, the first reference to the most controversial issue in dancehall had been made, without Anthony B saying anything. His set continued as he embodied a firebrand of outrageous moves and thrilling sounds that had the crowd eating out of his hand.

Next up was another old dancehall hand. Ninja Man's entrance was full of drama from his appearance in a stylish white suit and fedora, trailed by a young man carrying an umbrella to shade him. His set was full of life, something he appeared to have paid for afterwards judging by his drained appearance and slow movements backstage. The Don Gorgon, as he is also known, used his performance to promote his One Umbrella organisation aimed at reducing violence in Jamaica. Ninja believes that he can reduce crime in Jamaica by 60% within a year. Sadly, events have shown that to have been a little over optimistic.

These dancehall artists are primarily entertainers, something you couldn't really say about some of the bland, navel gazing, self-absorbed bands we are currently producing in the U.K. It is incredible that a country as small as Jamaica has such a prolific output of original talent.

Mavado

Elephant Man is the cartoon-iest of all the aforementioned cartoon characters. Just watching him would be enough as he arrived in a white cowboy suit and hat with some sort of Davy Crockett era weapon on his back. His hair was died several different colours and his performance was high on energy, most notably on one of his biggest hits, *Gully Creeper*.

He set the stage for what was to be the most anticipated section of the show. Bounty Killer and Mavado are members of a group of artists known as the Alliance. The Alliance is set up in competition to other dancehall stars, most notably Beenie Man. Consequently, the running order of Bounty Killer, Mavado, and then Beenie Man looked set to be mired in controversy. It did not disappoint. Mavado, the self-proclaimed Gully God, was the first of the explosive triumvirate to perform arriving on the stage at 3.27 a.m. Dressed all in white he cut a striking figure as he tore through a set comprised of his biggest hits. He paused briefly to, ironically given the slant of some of his lyrics, condemn the shottas responsible for violence against women and children. The set then reached a climax with *On the Rock* and *We Shall Overcome* with Mavado backed by a choir similarly dressed all in white. It was a stunning finale and he looked set to be the evening's stand out performer. In absolute juxtaposition, Bounty Killer arrived onstage dressed all in black. Bounty seems to revel in his bad boy persona and he is a cartoon villain in the Dick Dastardly tradition. His set was awesome and his presence menacing. The crowd were brimming with adulation as he moved towards his performance climax.

And then it happened.

Something seemed to snap in the Five Star General/Warlord, and he plummeted into a tirade of abuse and expletives aimed at other artists. He began by attacking Ninja Man, or more appropriately, Ninja Man's son, who was rumoured to be gay. This was a below the belt shot that some in the crowd frowned upon, and they ensured Bounty heard their disapproval. This only seemed to anger him further and he began a vicious attack on Beenie Man, containing numerous references to 'fish', which in Jamaica is another term for 'batty bwoy' or 'chi chi man', all homophobic terms of abuse. The crowd, who had been overwhelmed by what had been until this point a brilliant performance, turned on Bounty as one. The boos and whistles were furious, and it was made clear to the performer that they had heard enough. He finally exited the stage accusing all those who booed him of also being 'fish'. The reaction of the crowd and the Sumfest organisers, who issued an apology to the crowd immediately, should hold some encouragement for those right-minded souls appalled by homophobia. The crowd was not impressed by this low point of the evening and it was disappointing given the brilliance of Bounty's set. I didn't get a chance to challenge Bounty since the drama continued backstage with Killer being charged for the use of indecent language and escorted from the site by the police. He would later be given a court hearing date which he would fail to turn up to. Despite the tone that had been hit, it cannot be denied that this was a moment of high drama and something for the chattering classes to dissect on their way home. Backstage, Mavado was moving about angrily due to the treatment of his mentor. He gave a brief interview to MTV

Base before disappearing into the morning mist, refusing all other interview requests.

After all this drama, it was up to Beenie Man to rescue the evening/morning from leaving a bad taste in the mouth and save it he did. The sky was now light as the sun began visiting the Bay, yet Beenie ensured that the majority of the crowd did

not leave early to avoid the traffic with a consummate set befitting of one the island's most popular performers.

King of the Dancehall, Memories, Old Dawg, and *Dude* were dusted off and given new life in a highly energetic performance. Dressed in white, again contrasting with the villainous presence of Bounty, Beenie worked the stage with an effervescent and vibrant showing that emphasised just what a brilliant entertainer he is, but naturally he could not leave the Bounty controversy unanswered. He rather graciously absolved Bounty Killer by telling the crowd:

"Bounty, a de warlord, so 'im haffi war".

And so, as Beenie closed his set, the appraisals of Dancehall Night began.

For me personally, it was the best show I have ever seen. I don't remember having quite so many jaw-dropping moments as this event inspired. Every artist's entrance was accompanied by a real sense of anticipation, and some of the outfits worn were utterly unique. There was a thrilling vibe about the whole evening. It was exciting, lively, aggressive, and powerful, and in the Bounty/Beenie denouement, incredibly dramatic. Words are useless in trying to explain the sheer power of the show but asking myself whether Dancehall Night at Sumfest was "the Greatest Reggae Show on Earth", I would have to answer that tonight was the Greatest Music Show on Earth, period.

I was now on my last legs. I had been running between the stage and the media tent, as had 'my photographer', Poochie for almost ten hours, and whilst it was exhilarating, the toll would more than likely be felt on the forthcoming two nights. We both were desperate to get sleep, given that we had now been up for twenty-four continuous hours. By the time we had found Kelvin, negotiated the traffic, and got to our temporary home, it would be twenty-six hours. Twelve hours later we would be at it again.

Chapter Thirteen

Once More into the Breach

Three hours sleep. That is all I had. Due to the excitement of the previous night's show, the heat and the strange surroundings, three hours was all I could manage before Ras Kelvin came to pick us up for Day 2. He had come armed with a stool this time for the in-between set lulls. By all accounts, Poochie had managed a similar amount of sleep, so we waited, trying not to look like tramps despite a close approximation to the living dead. Tonight, would be International Night 1, the night when Sumfest introduces some talent from outside of Jamaica.

We left the villa an hour later than previously, partly because we did not want to be there first again, but also because Kelvin had overslept. When we arrived at the media tent, we were first there... again. The media tent is a strange affair. In the first section there is a supply of food and drink for the press. The second room is laid out with internet access and various ports for radio journalists to position themselves. For part of the evening, we were seated next to BBC Radio's Chris Goldfinger who is a lovely guy. He was in the minority, as most of the media present at Sumfest were like selfish and savage piranha fish. And yet even the media seemed to be outnumbered by freeloaders and hangers on. There were a few people within the tent and in the front of stage media section who seemed to do nothing all night except eat the food and make (mostly) failed attempts at trying to look cool. The third room is arranged exclusively for television interviews and contains comfy leather sofas and flowers. It was a nice set up. However, my lack of sleep and resultant growling demeanour meant that I was not in the best frame of mind for an evening with the type of people I would normally cross the road to avoid.

This night's show would be quite different from Dancehall Night. The artists lined up were of a more soulful and conscious nature than the fanfare of colour and controversy that was dancehall. The impressively dreaded Immanuel Walsh kicked off the evening with a set of sublime rootsy reggae. Pressure, Terry Linen, and Courtney John kept the standard high before Lutan Fyah appeared with a mightily impressive set, containing the wonderful *Africa*.

It was a constant challenge to be taking photographs of the performances and to be catching artistes for interview and as such I did not get to see whole sets by certain performers. What was worse was that my antique tape recorder had broken and so I was forced to make shorthand notes. It was for this reason that I missed LUST but was lucky enough to catch Queen Ifrica who was one of the highlights tonight. She delivered an excellent set of cultured tunes occasionally punctured by a bout of dancehall fyah! She was also responsible for the first mention of Bruce Golding's comments this evening, which she followed up with a song that was unequivocal in its negative stance on homosexuality.

By now I was finding the homophobia difficult to ignore and so when interviewing Queen Ifrica later I mentioned that Bruce Golding seemed to be a popular topic this weekend. She laughed and claimed that she found the furore surrounding his comments amusing, though she followed her comment up by saying that:

"We have to acknowledge who we are and live together. Homosexuals are human beings too we just have to find a balance".

The interview with Queen Ifrica was one of the best because she is a thoughtful and intelligent woman who was highly gracious with her time, yet on this issue I was still left wondering where she really stood.

It was also around this time that my temper had begun to fray a little. When you are surrounded by journalists all wanting a piece of an artist, it appears manners, morals and that great British institution, the queue, go out of the window. Consequently, I had been continually bumped and bashed in my attempts to speak to some of the artistes and I had had enough. This aggression would not stand. The first incident that had made my temperature rise involved one of the hangers on. I had seen this guy near us all evening seemingly paying a great deal of interest in Poochie. He was dressed in what looked like a pair of plus fours, and his hairstyle suggested that he had spent far too much time in the mirror, an item I suspect he found trouble tearing himself away from. He then began to indulge in something that I have found rather disconcerting in Jamaican society. Some Jamaican men seem to look upon women as pieces of meat. I don't mean in the sense of a Saturday night meat market nightclub in Britain where guys stare from a distance. These men seem to examine women close up, in their faces, as if they are weighing up the value of prized heifer. This 'farmer' was soon rebuffed by Poochie who told him she was married. I was unaware of this incident, but it seemed that Poochie was not at all happy with what had occurred. My initial response would have been to take my now defunct tape recorder and shove it up his hoop, but I sensed my surroundings and valiantly succeeded in keeping my temper in check, for now. It is quite different from the fun and playful approach of the likes of Buzzy and Radar who don't take 'the chase' too seriously, this is altogether a little more menacing. When Poochie and I chatted about this later she explained that the pawing and drooling that this inadequate had indulged in, was in fact low level and that it can be far worse. It is a distasteful and misogynist practice and for me is as bad as the homophobia that exists on the island. It seems that some men in Jamaica flirt cheekily with a sense of fun, not at all seriously and fully expect to be rebuffed but it seems a section of the male population can come across as real sexual predators and it makes for very uncomfortable viewing. Back to the show and Keyshia Cole had been performing while this occurred and she looked to have put on a gritty performance. However we had to watch her on the screens in the media lounge area because we were still waiting to talk to returning artistes, she not being one of them incidentally. She must have been too big for JA. Incidentally, where is she now? This night's highlight for me was Jah Cure. As a resident of Montego Bay you could tell that he really wanted to put on a show. Jah Cure has incredible stage presence, a fabulous voice and supreme songwriting skills, but the throbbing bass at the front of the stage and the low level of Cure's mic meant that the sound was dreadful. It had been faultless all night, so it was a shame that Jah Cure did not benefit from the same high quality. Some of his songs are a journey from the great lovers' rockers of the 1970's all the way to Tamla and specifically Marvin. His performance, despite the sound, was spell-bounding and great in the true sense of the word. He was a miserable bugger backstage though and I couldn't be bothered with it and binned him off after a couple of non-committal answers. Maybe it was the sound problems or quite possibly fatigue but he was curt, short and borderline aggressive as he answered questions. In this respect he seems to be the closest thing Reggae has to Liam Gallagher, and that is not a compliment. His performance had been the closest you are likely to get to Bob Marley without it coming over as pastiche. However, due to his incarceration and problems with the law, questions over his credentials as Ras will remain. Having been arrested in 1999 and serving several years in prison on charges for gun possession, robbery and rape, it is sad to report that was again handed down a six year sentence in 2022 for stabbling a music promoter in the stomach whilst in Amsterdam. And yet Jah Cure is a star and he may well have gone on to become a superstar, but it appears that his suspect personality means his talent has been wasted.

While we had been waiting for Jah Cure to appear in the media tent, Keyshia Cole had finished, and we had been watching Akon on the big screen. For many, Akon was the highlight of this night. Three quarters of the way through his performance, the Senegalese star jumped the media barrier, ran through the VIP section, and scaled the fence. He then descended into the crowd to be with the people. This was great news for everyone. The audience got to see their hero up close, Sumfest got some great (and deserved) publicity, and the television cameras captured a spectacular moment. Yes, it was great news for everyone; everyone except for Ras Kelvin. On our way home he seemed sulkily quiet and when asked why he bemoaned the fact that when Akon jumped down into the public area, he landed rather heavily on something of Kelvin's.

"Akon man, him a mash up mi stool", (with accompanying teeth sucking).

Despite his seat having been splintered into tiny pieces, Kelvin had loved the performance because in terms of drama it was up there with the Bounty controversy of the previous night. Yet some less charitable in the media tent were suggesting that there was a reason for Akon's escapades (he went on to scale the sound mixing scaffolding before rather clumsily zip lining down it). Someone in the media tent commented "He ain't no Spiderman", meaning the escapade may have been to do with a less than hot reception.

Meanwhile, I was packing away by the screen when another of those hangers-on, told me to sit down in no uncertain terms. I responded in kind as did Poochie and his response once more smacked of misogyny. He turned his fingers on an imaginary radio dial and muttered "click" to her.

"I can think of something that rhymes with that" I responded nodding towards him. This seemed to confuse him, and he sloped away.

It seems the lessons of Pankhurst and the Suffragette Movement have yet to reach Jamaica. I was just hoping that I could get through tomorrow and forget the non-existence of manners in this quagmire of bad attitude.

Akon's performance was entertaining then and was a real talking point for the crowd, who were threatening to drift away until Richie Spice arrived. This is the real graveyard slot at Sumfest and yet to be fair to Sumfest, they have ensured that the evening's ending is with a local star. But even Beenie's crowd the previous night had begun to drift away when they sensed the end was nigh, and so it is an uphill battle keeping them there. Richie Spice coped admirably not least because songs such as *The World Is a Cycle* and *Di Plane Land* are belters. The veteran Cocoa Tea was meant to be closing the evening's proceedings, but he protested that the international stars should fill the last slot, not the Jamaicans, so chose not appear.

We had packed up anyway and were sloping back to Kelvin's van. Whilst not hitting the heights of Dancehall Night, the International Night had still offered plenty of thrills and spills, notably onto Ras Kelvin's stool. I just felt that I needed sleep desperately.

Chapter Fourteen

The End of the Greatest Reggae Show in the World

International Night 1 had been very good indeed, but it was still a shadow of the explosive first night. After the second night I had managed six hours sleep. By my calculation that means I have had nine hours sleep in seventy-two hours. I feel and look as rough as hell. Well, rougher than normal.

Jamaica it seems was also suffering, given the amount of rain that was coming down. At one point it seemed unlikely that the final night would go ahead (and I was secretly hoping for a 24-hour postponement just so I could recuperate), but then at six o' clock p.m., a tickertape message ran across the bottom of the Jamaican News Channel. Sumfest would be going ahead despite the weather conditions. These conditions included the threat of flash-flooding and so I was not sure about the wisdom in heading off to a field by the sea with such warnings ringing in my ears. My feet and legs ached but I decided I was determined to complete the experience if only to see Etana whose vibe I have liked for some time through reading the limited press devoted to her and generally reggae in the UK. I also had my suspicions she might just steal the show tonight.

When we arrived at the Catherine Hall Entertainment Complex, it was more like the Glastonbury Festival in England. I had not envisaged coming to a music event in Jamaica and traipsing around in thick mud, but that is exactly what I got. When we entered the tent Poochie pointed to where I had been positioned the previous night and told me that my plug socket had been removed. After my frustrations the previous night I marched defiantly over to where the new incumbents sat and demanded that my plug be reinstated. I

Etana

then squinted (no contact lenses) to see that my plug was still in the socket. I looked at the huge man to whom I had been directing my anger, and sheepishly tip-toed back to the obviously myopic Poochie murmuring things like "Yeah...don't mess with my plug man, let that be a lesson...." and other such 'I made a right fool of myself there' masking platitudes. The BBC was no longer there. Maybe they had got enough material on nights one and two or maybe they did not want to be associated with the English-accented, manners crusader seated by their side: CAPTAIN PLEASE AND THANK YOU: The Well-Mannered Superhero from the UK! My crusade had obviously failed as whilst patiently queuing for the Touchstone Productions overworked and tired staff to print off the appearance times for the evening, the manager of an abomination to the purity of Reggae (who shall remain nameless) sent me sprawling halfway across the room whilst jumping the queue. Apology? Don't be stupid. This time it was my trusty sidekick, MISS DON'T TAKE NO SHIT, who assailed the woman for her rudeness. She eventually turned, looked me in the eye and issued an "I'm Sorry" that was dripping with malice. Oh Dear. This evening looked set to contain the same stresses of the night before.

Still there was music to be heard. Roots Underground opened with a lively set. Andy Vernon gave the concert an acoustic vibe, before Bonafide, four brothers, began to crank things up a little. And then came tonight's moment I had been waiting for. Etana's entrance was befitting of a great reggae diva in the pure superstar meaning of the word. She is pretty, has a belting voice and is capable of chirping through lovely ballads and equally adept at attacking tunes with real aggressive emotion. Her performance tonight is an amalgamation of all these factors, and her confidence is high. This is a performer coming of age and one born for the stage. She entered wearing a wonderful dress that, being a man, I can't describe too well. It was black with a silver, glittery guitar across the midriff. The dress ended at the knees in a flurry of green and red with material that looked like crepe paper (a brief discussion in Pleasanton the following day with all the female members of the household who had been watching on T.V. came to a consensus that it was a mesh-like material). I still knew no better. Finally, the back was tied up in beautiful gold laces. Etana is proud of her Rasta faith, and she was ensuring we were reminded of it in the most glamorous of ways. Her set was superb. She mixed reggae and soul and got the crowd moving in time to her powerful songs. Standouts were the obvious and wonderful *I Am Not Afraid* and *Jah Chariot* which reminds me of an old The Congos classic. Every song was attacked with gusto and zeal. She moved around the stage with ease; an echo of Tina here, a dash of Aretha there, but always reminiscent of the great reggae singers of the past such as her beloved Aunt, Marcia Griffiths. Etana's between song banter was modest and heartfelt. She explained how on her way to Montego Bay the car she had been travelling had spun off one of the sopping wet roads, but that everyone had been fine. She put her safe appearance at Sumfest down to the Almighty Jah Rastafari! Etana, as her hit song suggests, is not afraid to speak out either. Proud mother that she is, she launched into a blistering attack on the state of the world today. She talked about nuclear proliferation and war, and then added:

"Young men are coming home with no limbs, coming home and committing suicide, coming home mentally deranged. NOT MY SON!"

The Wailers would have been proud. It contrasted with much of what we had been hearing all weekend and was therefore quite refreshing. As she left the stage to a fantastic reception, she was passed some red roses which only further added to the aura of a modern-day diva. In interview she proved equally charming. I was looking down at my notes as she first passed me and on naturally looking up she twittered a "Hi!" She bounced around the interview room always smiling, always gracious, before arriving at my desk. Her answers to my questions (which were carefully listened to) elicited some of the best responses of the three days (along with both Queen Ifrica and Anthony B). She seems extremely modest about her natural talent but I can see her moving onto great things.

The evening continued with female duo Brick & Lace who by all accounts are starting to make waves stateside. The name 'Brick & Lace' sounds like a U.K. cabaret act from the seventies, the type of band who sang dire and cheesy cover songs. The songs they had did not stand out to me, I thought their look was dated, and I simply didn't get 'it', whatever 'it' is. Meanwhile, whilst sitting back in the press area, some American guy with a beard that made you think that perhaps some people shouldn't grow beards, picked up my pen from off my desk and began to walk away with it. Now pens are a valuable commodity in the media tent, especially to someone such as I who is always putting them down and leaving them places, and having already lost a few I was not prepared to watch my penultimate pen disappear into the distance.

"You're welcome", I muttered sarcastically. Apology? Fat chance.

"I need to use it and I saw you had one in your hand" he replied.

"Well, it is polite to ask", came back CAPTAIN PLEASE AND THANK YOU.

"Do you know what" mused the American, "I am just going to put your precious pen down here for you".

"Why, Thank You", I replied.

He then spewed out a barely audible expletive whilst giving me a death stare, to which I caustically responded, "Get a shave". My lack of sleep was beginning to reveal itself.

Next up was Tarrus Riley who performed several of his mellifluous hits and invited his dad Jimmy onto the stage to join him for a special Sumfest moment. He had the crowd in his hand but was not quite as in control of them as the magnificent Beres Hammond. Everybody in Jamaica loves Beres, especially the ladies, and I have never heard anyone say a bad word against him. Now of veteran status, he commands authority and his set tonight was a wonderful sing-along for most of the crowd. By the time he was finished I was packed up and ready to go.

This meant I would miss T-Pain and Lil Wayne, but they weren't reggae and that was all I was here to see and more importantly, I was shattered. We went and sat by the main gate where the police were stationed and tried to get hold of Kelvin by phone but repeatedly failed. Every ten minutes we did this for the whole of T-Pain's set and for most of Lil' Wayne's. I even went looking for him because we had initially seen him on the big screen and given his height and his enormous wrap we assumed he would be easy to track down, but he was nowhere to be seen.

It turned out that he had gone to sleep in his van. When he finally woke up and saw the 237 missed calls, he came to meet us. We had decided to say farewell to the amazing Reggae Sumfest out of fatigue, even though we would miss a personal favourite, the wonderful John Holt.

And so, my first ever Sumfest was over.

The Sumfest experience was one to treasure. The organisers offered up a stunning bill of the biggest names in Reggae, save for a few noticeable absentees such as Buju Banton and Sizzla. To that they added a sprinkling of international stars and some old school performers of note to create a wonderful package. There is something for everyone at Sumfest and it is run with cool and friendly efficiency. It was, in all honesty, the most spectacular and colourful event I have ever witnessed, especially as it thrives on the wonderful and comical crowd participation of the people of Jamaica. I cannot imagine a better festival.

When I was dropped off by Kelvin, I managed to get three more hours sleep in the villa before we were turned out. As we sat outside waiting for my Rasta friend's return, an enormous piece of fruit fell from a tree onto the reception roof from where it proceeded to roll down before dropping with force onto my weary head. I heard it, I guessed it was coming my way, but simply did not have the energy to move away from its trajectory. I don't think the owner of the villas had ever heard such language. After the thrills, spills, and excitement of a marvellous three days, I couldn't wait to get back to Pleasanton, get back to my family, get back to the food, and most importantly, get back to my bed.

Even CAPTAIN PLEASE AND THANK YOU needs sleep.

Chapter Fifteen

"Marcus Garvey's Words Come To Pass..."

Reggae Sumfest was a (Bounty) killer. As such, I was feeling half dead and spent the next few days recovering. I was back in Pleasanton, and Momma and Pops were trying to coax some life out of me to no avail. On occasional forays outside the haven of my bedroom I would bump into fellow zombie Poochie who would also strain to raise anything in acknowledgement before sloping back to her room. Once recovered, everyone wanted to know the gossip. A whole day at least was spent explaining the ins and outs of Bounty, Etana, Jah Cure, and Akon.

The following morning, I awoke to the announcement on Irie FM that it was 23rd July and more importantly H.I.M. Hailie Selassie's birthday. The gravitas with which this news was relayed made me realise just what a grip Rastafari still has on the island, and I was impressed that Jamaican culture continues to honour his role in their history.

Both before my trip and since I have spent time at the Twelve Tribes HQ in Manchester U.K. (I am a member and of the tribe of Zebulun) and so knew all of the important dates, but it was the fact that H.I.M.'s birthday plays such a vital role in the calendar of Jamaica that resonated especially since I was under the previous impression that many in Jamaica frown upon the Rastafarians. I continually felt myself being drawn to this way of life now I was able to see it in practice. It is not just about weed smoking, a Western created stereotype, and in fact the holy 'erb is mostly used as a conducive tool towards spiritual 'reasonings' which are discussions about the scriptures. Similarly the diet is Ital, healthy and salt free, and despite my lapses on this trip for reasons of politeness and propriety, it is in line with my own personal beliefs. Rastafari is bulit upon doing good unto others and waiting for destruction of the Babylonian 'shitstem' which has brought so much harm to the world, and via the colonial powers, to this fantastic island.

On this momentous day everyone was going into Claremont so I joined them in order to get some more shopping. One thing I have come to accept is that no-one is a rush to get anywhere quickly. Most mornings in the house consist of a three-hour sleepwalk before it bursts into life. I waited on the porch for everyone to finish their ablutions. I noticed that I no longer adopt the cowboy position with my back to the wall facing the front, and this might well be the result of receiving the welcome news that MACHETEMAN has "gone a foreign" - abroad.

With this in mind, and given my recent brushes with Jamaican misogyny, I decided I would give the Buzzy approach a go, mainly to try and impress Buzzy who was driving today. As we drove through the town of Moneague we passed a girl, and I leant out of the window and hissed "Heyyyyy sssssssssssssexy".

I looked to the driving Buzzy for appreciation, but he was of stern face and moved his eyes worriedly in the direction of the back seat. I turned laughingly towards the cheap seats to see a glare from Momma that could have frozen the Caribbean Seas.

She then bellowed the Golding-esque "Not in My Car!", and I shuffled about nervously in my seat for the rest of the journey.

The shopping expedition that we had set out on was just that, an expedition. There were five of us all around the trolley like a mini debating society discussing the various merits and debits of certain brands and their prices. Six people had initially arrived, but Pops had made the sensible move having spotted an acquaintance outside. He returned twenty-five minutes later to find that the trolley had advanced approximately six feet up the first aisle. After ninety or so minutes we had made it to the checkout, and I ruminated on the fact that the average soccer match takes less time. TJ, who had been running in, out, and around the supermarket like a lunatic, came up to us and explained that Buzzy was now outside chatting to somebody. Someone asked who to.

"I don't know, some girl" he replied innocently. Having packed, we made our way to the car. Suddenly, and out of nowhere, a recognizable face popped up. "Remember Me? it asked.

"Ah yes, it's you, Bob Marley!" I exclaimed remembering his face from my last visit to Claremont

I was genuinely pleased to see him, until he refused to move until I had given him some money. Before I had managed to delve into my pocket Pops had convinced him to move on in no uncertain fashion. I must give 'Bob Marley' some kudos if not dollars. He has a good scam going there. Introduce yourself in a non-threatening fashion that suggests that you are just a friendly local and then catch them off guard on their second visit by demanding money as a 'friend'.

Once the shopping was done, and given it was 23rd July, H.I.M.'s birthday, I considered it appropriate to visit the hometown of one of the heroes of the Rastafari movement.

St. Ann's Bay is the area from which one of the leading lights in black consciousness hails. Marcus Mosiah Garvey was born in St Ann's Bay on August 17th 1887. This great man was until more recently (and certainly in the West) a forgotten hero of Black emancipation and the quest for civil rights. Yet for me Marcus Mosiah Garvey should be on the same pedestal as the great heroes of the Civil Rights Movement such as Martin

Luther King and Malcolm X. Garvey formed the UNIA (Universal Negro Improvement Association) and was the originator of the Black Star Liner project which depending on your view was either aimed at shipping former slaves back to Africa in order to make the continent a seat of black autonomy, or was never a truly serious venture but simply served as a means of psychic relief and hope for the suffering former slaves in the Americas and the Caribbean. Whilst preaching his gospel in the United States, Garvey was pursued by J. Edgar Hoover and the nascent FBI. Hoover, who had previously sent a memo to another officer speaking of regret that Garvey had committed no crime whilst in the USA, finally managed to get his man on a trumped-up charge of mail fraud. Garvey never really recovered his standing following this incident and he died in exile in 1940 and was originally buried in Kensal Green Cemetery, London. His remains were later exhumed and taken to Jamaica where he was re-interredin the National Park on November 15th, 1964 and was proclaimed as Jamaica's first national hero. During the period in which Garvey was active, he invoked hostility from both white and black. He might have pointed them towards the words of Jonathan Swift who once wrote:

"When a great genius appears in the world the dunces are all in confederacy against him".

Garvey has been internationally rehabilitated of late, and not before time. Yet Garvey's memory lived on throughout those wilderness years in a religious group that has used his speeches and writings as their inspiration. To them he is John the Baptist and they are the Rastafarians, but it should also be noted that Marcus Garvey was far from enamoured with today's birthday boy H.I.M. Hailie Selassie. Nevertheless, these two, with Robert Nesta Marley form the holy trinity of the Rastafari faith.

As for St Ann's Bay, I was expecting a somnambulant little village, but the town is a lively and vibrant one, the busiest I have seen thus far (Kingston aside) and the noise of the place matches the movements. It is all hustle and bustle. The market is the hub of life and whilst walking through I was pressured to buy the most lethal looking but beautifully carved knife. Had MACHETEMAN still been on the scene I may have been tempted. Instead, I simply suggested that I wouldn't get it through customs much to the vendor's disappointment.

As we had entered St. Ann's Bay on the road from the hills, the first suggestion that this is Garvey's hometown is an enormous statue of the man outside the Primary School. From a distance the statue looks impressive, and I was anxious to see it up close. Sadly, on inspection it appears to need some care and attention. The inscription beneath the statue proclaims;

RIGHT EXCELLENT MARCUS MOSIAH GARVEY NATIONAL HERO BORN AUGUST 17, 1887 – DIED JUNE 10, 1940. The 't' of 'Right', and the 'l' of 'National' are both missing. Similarly, the junior school and library behind Marcus looked in need of some love also, and it is pleasing to know that the government was in the process of addressing these issues. On the wall to the left of Marcus's mount is written one of Garvey's quotes:

"WE DECLARE TO THE WORLD THAT AFRICA MUST BE FREE".

When the statue and its accompanying building are tidied up, the memorial should be befitting of the man. I nipped into the library behind the statue to ask if there were any leaflets on Garvey. One of the library assistants helpfully dug out three old pamphlets that seemed to be the sum-total of their archive

Marcus Garvey words come to pass

on him. In conversation with the gentleman I assumed to be the Head Librarian, he told me that Garvey was born at 32 Market Street in the town, so I made that my next destination. I should have taken oxygen and crampons, because the first, uphill, three quarters of Market Street has no houses on it, and it was with some consternation that I was out of breath on reaching number 2 Market Street. After a further climb and having negotiated some of the many bends in the road I paused outside a house to check that I was heading in the correct direction. A grey haired and lithe Rasta introduced himself as the owner of the house below which Garvey was born, and he told me that he was the custodian of the memorial site. He accompanied me further up the hill until we reached a beautiful and peaceful garden that stood upon the site where Garvey was born. A huge turquoise mural with Marcus's image and a set of four quotes marks the area. A flag bearing the colours red, black, and green flutters in applause for the great man. It is a recognisable flag because it is now used across the globe, especially at times when the Black Lives Matter movement is on the march. It is known as the Pan-African flag and the UNIA flag, and given his energy and blazing determination it is no surprise that it was designed by Garvey himself. The flag was created in response to the shocking racist song from the early 1900s entitled "Every Race Has a Flag but the Coon". The colours represent the colour of the blood shed for freedom, the colour and pride of black people, and the colour of the lush vegetation of Africa. To the right of the wall are two information placards, one detailing Marcus's life and the other showing the projected plans for this memorial. To the left of the mural is a metal plate boasting the site upon which Marcus was born. It was placed there "by a grateful nation" to mark the centenary of his birth. Perched above the plate is a red, black, and green columned plinth with a bust of a proud Marcus Garvey crowning the monument which was donated by the African Peoples Association. All these artefacts are surrounded by a stunning arrangement of flowers and flora, all green and pinks. My Ras guide went on to explain that when the PNP were in power they had projected plans to establish an archival centre here, but with their defeat in the election their plans have stalled somewhat. It is a shame because it would stand upon a hill with the most stunning vista of St. Ann's Bay, and it would be truly fitting to have a Marcus Garvey archive based there. Whilst I stood making eye contact with Marcus Mosiah Garvey, I pondered on what sort of man from such humble beginnings could make such a large impact on the world's consciousness both black and white? He must have had bravery beyond measure.

Before I left, the Rasta gave me his phone number and suggested I visit again before I leave Jamaica because he had much more to tell me. I was overwhelmed to have at been at the site of the birthplace of such a great man and as such I was pensive as we headed back to Pleasanton where I was to witness a new spectacle.

Today was the first day I have been a spectator to the unleashing of Fidel. This is because Fidel scares me. Fidel is the house dog, but he is not a little fluffy dog or a bouncy effervescent spirit pounding about the backyard. Fidel is a beast. I couldn't begin to imagine what breed he is, but he appears to be a cross between every vicious dog imaginable. His eyes say that he wants to kill, and every move made in his pound is accompanied by a blood curdling snarl. It was Buzzy who got him out. This was basically a full-on wrestling match as Buzzy battled with the collar and the pound door for approximately five minutes. On his release Fidel made desperate lunges at everyone before Buzzy got him under control and took him out for his walk. I pray he never gets loose.

Visiting the site of Marcus Garvey's birth gave me a thirst for more of the history of Jamaica. On hearing that we were to visit relatives in St. Thomas the next day I knew that we would be passing close to Morant Bay, and I hoped I could persuade one of the driving squad (a squad I still hoped to join in the near future) to make a detour into that town. Having visited the memorial dedicated to Garvey I wanted to visit the site where another great man is honoured.

Paul Bogle was a Baptist Deacon who, peaceable by nature, led the Morant Bay Rebellion and was killed during the ensuing slaughter in 1865. A statue of him stands outside the courthouse in Morant Bay and I felt it was imperative that I visit it.

Chapter Sixteen

96 Degerees In The Shade

Jamaica is not a big country. It is 230 km long (146 miles) with its width varying from 35 km (22 miles) to 81 km (51 miles). Given these statistics, I had (not unreasonably) imagined that to travel the length of the island would take approximately three hours. This optimistic projection did not however consider three variables. Firstly, the roads are a law unto themselves and do not know the meaning of "a straight line". Secondly, the drivers are nutcases. Thirdly, nothing is that simple in Jamaica.

We set off from Pleasanton and through the parish of St. Ann which I recently discovered is known as the 'Ganja Parish', although I once had a lengthy conversation with a fellow Welshman, the lovely and much-missed Howard Marks, about Jamaica and ganja (which he knew a thing or two about being at one time the biggest global exporter of said crop) and in his opinion St. Elizabeth has the best weed.

St Ann is all mountains and emerald scenery and as such it appears to be a land of mystery; as mysterious as its people can sometimes be, such is the impenetrable sound of the patois on some of those I meet in the parish. As we moved out of the winding and breath-taking scenery of St. Ann, we slipped into the flatter parish of St. Catherine. Despite its lack of mountainous wonder, the parish's roads are still lined with the most magnificent palm trees. Vegetable and fruit stalls manned by young machete wielding men and women add splashes of natural colour to the journey, with greens and yellows being the colours of note, again just like the flag. As we passed one chunk of greenery approaching the infamous Flat Bridge, Michael the mechanic, today's escort, once more mentioned the local legend that is a clump of rocks and trees shaped like a vagina. I was no nearer to finding it than when I first arrived. What I did see were gigantic trees that looked like huge menacing fingers striving to catch passing motorists. The country gave way to the villages and then we hit the outskirts of Spanish Town once again. The landscape is not too different to the rest of St. Catherine, but both the people and the town look tougher than the norm. Thankfully we were not accompanied by the pall of smoke that accompanied us last time, the landfill fire having been put out.

The outskirts of the town are clustered and cramped and fenced up with corrugated iron. The road is like a morbid pet shop; on this journey alone I have seen dead dogs, cats, frogs and rats. Today as we travelled into Kingston there were several cars selling items out of their trunks, their owners engaged in trading in a mobile market. The roadsides here are littered with rubbish and debris and it seems to be the norm to use the deep gullies that appear within minutes of each other as personal landfills. As we moved deeper into Kingston, Mo piped up in the back "Mavado, Mavado!" This five-year old's hero is Mavado who as previously mentioned is known as 'The Gully God'. The singer in fact comes from an area in a particularly ghettoised part of Kingston, Cassava Piece. The 'Gully' is a trench that must be crossed to get there. Poochie suggested that if her nephew would like to go and see him, he would be going alone. As we moved through the nether regions of the city, I noticed that it was practically empty. This could be for several reasons. Kingston might not have woken up on this Saturday morning as it was still early; this part of Kingston could have a high density of (the high number of) Sabbath Keepers who strictly observe the day almost identically to the Jewish tradition; or, and more ominously, the people might not like to be on the streets in this part of

Gun Court

Kingston. I think it is more likely to be the first case, but Kingston's reputation goes before it. That said I did later discover another use that some Kingstonians have for barrels. I overheard a conversation that suggested that this area of Kingston is where they sometimes find bodies in said vessels. On a similar theme, we then passed G.P., the General Penitentiary which houses the most notorious criminals in Jamaica. It might be a prison, but it has an amazing ocean view.

The shift from industrialised Kingston into St. Thomas was a welcome relief because St. Thomas is quite beautiful. The roads swim along, meandering lazily through the lushest of countryside and I reckon every plant imaginable to man must live in this parish. St. Thomas has history and legend by the bucket-load too. Barely into the parish we passed a simple monument to Three Fingered Jack, a slave of heroic stature, lying at the side of the road. Jack is believed to have used obeah to help him escape Jamaican slavery some time before 1780 and became a feared leader of a group of maroons (runaway slaves) but sadly he was eventually captured and killed. Indeed, St. Thomas is a stronghold of the dark arts of obeah so I vowed to be on my best behaviour. Minutes afterwards we are in Yallahs Pond where legend has it that two brothers were fighting over a piece of land when the waters came in and flooded it ensuring that neither would benefit from its fertile grounds. It must have been a damn big piece of land because the Pond is massive.

The roads are atrocious the further you move into the parish. Dusty road repairs make the journey even more uncomfortable but then I guess that is the price you pay for keeping your parish off the tourist map, which St. Thomas, save for occasional forays into the Blue Mountains, seems to have achieved judging by the empty beaches. The town of White Horses commands a striking cliff top view, and the people seem to contain several characters judging by the argument we chanced upon that seemed to include the whole village. There were about eighty people of all ages standing on both sides of the street, some observing, some chipping in, but everywhere was a blizzard of frantic hand gestures. It was like they had all arranged to assemble on the main road to have a bloody good argument before retiring for a Red Stripe and a toke on the 'erb. Who knows, they may have just been discussing the weather.

Exiting the town and moving into Roselle there is a timely reminder of the perils of driving in Jamaica. A metal fence that skirts the cliff side has one absent panel and a bundle of yellow tape in its place, suggesting that someone had misjudged the bend. Another road hazard I have noticed aside from potholes and suicidal drivers, is fruit. Occasionally the driver will have to swerve to avoid an enormous and randomly placed breadfruit or melon. The road in Roselle is barely two-way but is a road that slices you through that place where the sea ends, and the mountains begin. On one side the endless Caribbean waters gently coax you along whilst the Blue Mountain's cascading fountains guide you protectively through this sumptuous scenery. The Goodyear factory, all derelict rust and weather-beaten decay, sits just outside of Roselle. I would have thought Goodyear would have been thriving here given the state of the roads and the attitude to

Paul Bogle - a Colossus of Jamaica

driving. In fact, the number of potholes we discovered on this journey alone, everyone accompanied by a metallic clunk, would have persuaded me to buy shares in a tyre company in Jamaica.

I suddenly saw how close we were to Morant Bay and put in my request to visit. It was not met with total agreement within the van given that the cargo consisted of disinterested kids and adults who have passed Paul Bogle's statue daily at some point in their lives since most of my family are proud sons and daughters of this parish. Nevertheless, I was indulged, and soon found myself facing the impressive statue of Paul Bogle.

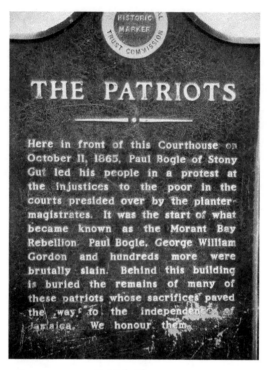

THE PATRIOTS

Here in front of this Courthouse on October 11, 1865, Paul Bogle of Stony Gut led his people in a protest at the injustices to the poor in the courts presided over by the planter magistrates. It was the start of what became known as the Morant Bay Rebellion. Paul Bogle, George William Gordon and hundreds more were brutally slain. Behind this building is buried the remains of many of these patriots whose sacrifices paved the way to the independence of Jamaica. We honour them.

British Shame

Designed by Edna Manley, a renowned sculptor as well as First Lady and later mother of a Prime Minister, he stands about ten feet tall with legs astride and dwarfed by impressive shoulders whilst clasping a sword in both hands with a determined look on his face. As I scrambled all over the statue and the decrepit courthouse behind, my family took on refreshments and left me to explore every part of this historical site.

My enthusiasm had blinded me to the approach of a tall and serious looking man who I later came to discover was the magnificently named Herpaul Lincoln. Mr. Lincoln introduced himself as the curator of the site and my doubts about his authenticity were soon brushed aside as he began to unload the most impressive information about what took place here. Morant Bay had previously been a Spanish colony for 100 years but when the English failed to wrestle control of Cuba from the Spanish, they took Morant Bay as a consolation prize. In 1865 Paul Bogle, a man of God, led a poverty-stricken protest which was met with British gunfire and the deaths of twenty-eight people. The courthouse was razed to the ground, probably to the condition it looks in today. The British response to the attempted rebellion was one of absolute evil savagery. Thousands of men and women were flogged and over four hundred rebels, including Paul Bogle of Stony Gut, were executed. Where I was stood was where this act of brutality occurred and it was chilling to be conscious of that fact. With this, Herpaul turned on his feet and began walking through the derelict courthouse whilst still talking to me. I followed and looking back noticed the huddle of meerkats taking drinks by the car looking in my direction. Slowly but surely, they approached like little creatures wondering whether they should venture quite so far.

Behind the courthouse was an amazing but hidden historical site. Three huge cannons point out to the stunning ocean in what is Morant Fort. Here also are memorials to those who were brutally murdered by the British. One is beautifully worded. It proclaims:

IN REMEMBRANCE OF PAUL BOGLE, GEORGE WILLIAM GORDON AND THE 437 MARTYRS OF OCTOBER 1865 WHO FELL BECAUSE THEY LOVED FREEDOM. IN GRATITUDE FROM THE GENERATIONS WHO NOW WITNESS THAT THEY DID NOT DIE IN VAIN.

Another states:

HERE IN JUNE 1965 WERE UNCOVERED THE LAST
REMAINS OF THE MARTYRS OF OCTOBER 1865.

Herpaul told me that Paul Bogle has been identified as one of
them due to his wearing of a gold tooth that was still in his
skull.

By now I had been joined by most of the family, some
professing total ignorance of the existence and nature of this
place despite their having passed it every day. Herpaul and I
began discussing slavery in general and he suggested that the
British have had a bad press. He claimed that the British had
contributed to acts of humanity in the region for instance in
the education of slave children. I told him I wasn't convinced.
Whilst completing my undergraduate degree I was taught by
Dr Michael Tadman whose theory of 'key slaves' is one I
support. In short, he considers those acts of altruism to be a
form of psychic relief for the slave owner. In treating house
slaves well (whilst showing only cruelty to the field slaves) the
slave owners could consider themselves good people. I
thanked and tipped Herpaul, got in the car, and was quiet for
some time afterwards.

Our next stop was to Jay's to pick up some of his belongings.
Jay lives through Top Pen and the public road up to the
houses is astonishing. Palm trees lean over the road to hold
hands whilst those not as deeply in love wave and whisper
sweet nothings to each other. Climbing higher still and north
of Morant Bay we creaked to loftier sights in the hill's heights,
sharing the road with goats and cows. We were in proper
'country'. We entered a village square where the car suddenly
stopped, and the family bundled out into hugs and kisses from
all those present. Everyone knew everyone and it was like the
arrival of celebrities. It was beautiful. The welcome for me was
heart-warming too. There was no element of the

(understandable) suspicion or distrust that I have very occasionally observed elsewhere, just a really cheerful "Wha' gwaan?" All of this took place in, and all over the heart of the village and so it was like watching that rare commodity, a feel-good soap opera.

After about an hour of everyone swapping stories, news, scandal, and generally just checking each other out and yelling things like "Yuh put on weight!", the cavalry moved up to Poppa's. Poppa (to Poochie and DeeDee) is an energetic looking pensioner dressed in a cool pair of shorts, de rigueur string vest, and bandana clamped to his head. He was grinning permanently throughout the time we were there. His house is beautifully quaint and idyllic, but incredibly hardy for a man of his approaching years. As if to confirm this, a torrential downpour unleashed itself whilst we were there. I was reminded of the 'Jah Rastafari!' story when the thunder took hold, but the Almighty Jah must have mislaid his camera today since there was no lightning. There was barely enough room for everyone in Poppa's house, which was clinically clean and tidy but seemingly lacking in the everyday things that we take for granted, and so feeling a little claustrophobic I ventured out into the garden and into the rain. The sweet rain, much needed, poured into a garden that was a rainforest. At times like this, one can really *feel* Nature. Another hour passed with me breathing in the sweet scent of the real Jamaica whilst everyone else caught up with their news and then we were on the move again.

Within fifteen minutes we had reached Bath Fountain. I had been told of a spring with healing powers and with my hypochondria on full alert I considered I had a list of ailments that needed the touch of a miracle cure. As we pulled up, we were confronted by a scrum of young men all swarming around us and wrestling to ensure that it was they who took us to the spring. This then developed into one of those now familiar Jamaican arguments. It was highly heated but never quite developed into the fist fight it threatened to. And so it was that our group of ten was escorted to the Fountain by three Alpha male Jamaicans.

The first thing to negotiate was the beautiful rope bridge suspended across the river before beginning the climb up through the glorious bush to where the spring was. When we reached the spring area there was a little blue tent erected, only big enough for a couple of people, which functioned as a changing room. Once stripped, except for a pair of natty white football shorts, I began the descent into the stream. The water was cold, and I wondered if the heat of this water was as incredible as I had been led to believe. The riverbed under my feet was hard and glazed in tiny rocks that hurt to walk on. I was led to an area with a particularly large rock and told by my guide (who incidentally had the most enormous feet that appeared to have been borrowed from a lion or a bear) to sit down. He then took a bucket with little holes punched into it, dipped it into the trough to my right side, and poured the contents onto my head. My language would have been far worse had I not been in polite company because the water was scalding (I later discovered that it was 130 degrees, and I did not doubt the precision of that temperature reading for one minute). My guide/torturer took my towel, dipped it in the trough and slammed it onto my back. Was he getting some sort of perverse kick from this? It was further slapped onto my legs, around my trunk, and wrapped around my, by now, scorching head. It was whilst I could see little else, having been blinded by the towel, that I looked down into my lap and embarrassingly discovered that my choice of swimwear had been a faux pas; my shorts were now practically transparent and my junk was on show for all to see. At least my guide did not notice as he then began slapping the top of my head with the fiery waters. I asked if it was a cure for premature baldness but was ignored. I had forgotten that in Jamaica people take things like this very, very seriously. As the sadist poured water over my head once more, he began the incantation,

"The father...the son..." and with each holy figure, he poured.

"And the Holy Spirit?" I second guessed, anxious that he finish his pouring as soon as possible.

"And the Holy Ghost" replied my guide disdainfully and solemnly with one, strangely more forceful pour.

He then asked me to stretch my back over the rock before beating me senseless in what passed for a massage. Everything was pummelled, stretched, twisted, and turned and I was left exhausted by an assault from massive hands and fiery water. Onto my front and the same again, only this time with Pimento Seed oil plastered all over me. I was then asked to sit up before two more hot buckets were passed over my head, and then a final cold one...the swine. I was then pointed towards a pipe stretching over the river out of which water sprinkled. I waded through the cold waters, trying to hide the front of my shorts whilst appearing not to be hiding the front of my shorts, only to discover that the pipe was churning out that viciously hot stream also. It really is quite amazing that a natural source can produce water of such heat. After wading back to the blue tent and re-establishing a sense of dignity to my nether regions I began to mentally imagine how much my massage might have cost, because, needless to say, it would not be free and I was right to imagine that a bout of haggling might ensue. This was one of those situations where I should have asked the price first.

The initial claim was astronomical, but I managed to barter them down by claiming to have no more money than the Jamaican $5000 I had in my pocket. This was taken, somewhat miserably before I was once more led back through a picture postcard over the bridge and into the car. Feeling bloody and bruised yet strangely energised, we left Bath Fountain and headed towards home but not before dropping in on some more folks and relatives who were having something of a family gathering. As we pulled up outside a small marquee tent I could see adults and children running all over the place. Someone was chopping sugar cane, another busting out coconuts with a machete, and another gutting fish.

Whilst there, I was surprised to hear one of the guests described as a "brown man". This seemed incongruous because in the politically correct Western world if someone had used such a description they would have been pilloried. However, in a country where the majority ethnicity is 92% per cent black, the terms 'brown man', 'white man', 'coolie man' (mixed race Indian) are not meant in a derogatory fashion, they are innocently used as adjectives to help those chatting recognise who is being talked about. Indeed, some family members have been described as 'brown' as a result of their having fairer skin. It is not taken as an insult. In fact, Jamaican men have a delectation for 'brown' girls (in the ring perhaps) which is not a measure I subscribe to, or particularly approve of, but it is not unusual in cultures other than Jamaica too. It also helps explain the culture of 'bleaching' whereby some women (and the occasional man) buy products aimed at lightening the skin, not always to good effect.

The women here meanwhile were all busily fussing about getting food ready as I was led to the house behind the marquee. The house was a much smaller version, but had a similar vibe to the house in Coppola's Godfather when the glory days of the Corleones have ended and the building was a run-down version of its former self. Perched atop a mini cliff-side the house looked like it could once have been a glorious home. Poochie took me to the water's edge where the vast Sea could be viewed flowing towards and then tipping over the horizon.

"This used to be Bustamante's house" she told me.

Sir Alexander Bustamante had presided over Jamaica's Independence in 1962, and ensured that it was a peaceful transition and as such he is also one of the country's national heroes. I was therefore disappointed that this house and its grounds had been allowed to fall into some state of disrepair, yet despite the damage it retained an earthy charm. With a little money and a lick of paint it is likely that it could be restored to its former glory.

In two days, I had swept through two centuries and a land of heroes. From Paul Bogle to Marcus Garvey to Sir Alexander Bustamante. I had been made aware of the struggle that Jamaica engendered to become what she is today. The people are poverty-stricken, but they are free as a result of the actions of these three great men amongst others. What Jamaica needs now are more heroes to move them out of the Third World and into a land of peace and exciting prospects, she certainly has the natural tools. Hopefully a new hero will soon come from within or without the political class to steer this island towards the kind of future these wonderful people deserve.

Chapter Seventeen

Kingston Town

I am unwell. Since I arrived in Jamaica I have had a hacking cough which has no doubt been exasperated by my constant smoking of cigarettes and weed. I am the type of person who constantly needs to be doing something and given the lethargic pace of Jamaican life at times, I have smoked an awful lot since being here. On hearing that Jay would be visiting the doctor, (not Beenie Man but a real man of medicine) I decided to tag along in the hope that if I coughed long and loud enough the doctor might prescribe me something, as well as the real patient. Once in the car and out of Pleasanton I discovered that the visit required a trip to Kingston because the doctor being consulted is an orthopaedic specialist and not a cough specialist, so it looked like I would have to keep availing myself of Doctor Pops and his weed/rum elixir – which I was starting to quite enjoy.

The trip began at 10 a.m. because we needed to get to Kingston and book in before the appointment, which was to take place "between 2 p.m. and 6 p.m.". I was simply excited to be moving into the real Kingston. I had been looking forward to a trip to the big city having spent most of my time in the countryside. As we approached the outskirts of the city, I saw the familiar docks which had been the closest I had got to Kingston thus far. We then shifted through built up Kingston 10 which seemed quite industrialised before reaching Kingston 5 where the people were moving in a seething, random mass. Kingstonians move at a faster pace than the rest of the country and the city itself was awash with business suits mixed in with the usual super-cool fashions. Everywhere the traffic crawled as we passed through Half Way Tree (where my beloved Spice Buns that I buy at home come from) and Cross Roads areas, as the citizens of Kingston dipped and ducked in and out of the impatient cars and went about their lives. It looked fabulous and I wanted to get right into the middle of it, but I seemed to be under virtual car arrest. My family would not let me out of the car until we turned into the hospital car park. There seemed to be an inbuilt fear about the place but from what I could see, I reckoned it was probably just like any tough city across the globe, be that Liverpool, New York, or Moscow all of which I have visited and survived (you might think surprisingly).

The hospital looked like an old-fashioned sanatorium. It was a neat and tidy building sitting on the border of a quiet park. We found the Doctor's office and checked in with the receptionist at 1.15pm. Despite arriving 45 minutes early, we were still sixth in line. The receptionist was typical of receptionists across the globe. She was a little Hitler in control of her own private Nazi Germany. If a tricky question arose, her response was to mutter disparaging remarks about the patients to herself before she jotted down their names in a notebook entitled *Slated for Destruction* (I may have lied about this). It was hard to fully comprehend what her role was in the hospital because she rarely turned her focus away from the barrage of personal calls she answered on her mobile phone. We decided to return at about 2.30 p.m. when we figured those in front of us might have been seen. In the meantime, after a toss-up between Tastee, Mother's, and Juici Patties, we devoured the latter's delicious fare to keep us sustained for the long haul that is a doctor's waiting room.

When we returned a guy in a wheelchair was holding court, and he held that court for about an hour, after which time the initial laughter that everyone had greeted his comments with became silent and stale as he refused to shut up and chatted non-stop and at length. When another patient finally took offence at one of the political comments made by WHEELCHAIRGUY, the latter only raised his voice higher, claiming that he was the font of all knowledge and that even Prime Ministers and politicians had agreed that he should be running the country.

I, meanwhile, was losing the will to live.

It was tiresome and only ended when the Prime Minister in waiting was wheeled in to see the Doctor. By now it was 3.30 p.m., and we were still only fourth in line. What was the doctor doing in there I wondered? Maybe the patients come in feeling ill and he operates there and then under the maxim "No Time Like the Present".

I was hoping that he might see fit to stitch WHEELCHAIRGUY's mouth up. For those of you thinking "How cruel, the poor man is in a wheelchair" I have two things to say;

1) You weren't subjected to his inane and offensive ramblings

2) You can still be disabled and an arsehole.

After a further interminable wait we were ushered in at 5 p.m., three hours after we had arrived, and I was thinking "this doctor had better be a genius".

We were guided into his office by Adolf whose sullen demeanour was strangely less evident around him. The doctor was male; slight of build, bald of head, and he had a tufty piece of facial hair supporting his chin. He asked Jay what the problem was and was told that it was scoliosis. The doctor asked how he knew, which seemed to be a pointless question given that the doctor had Jay's file and that the problem had been diagnosed about three months prior to this visit. Jay patiently replied that he had seen a doctor in April who had told him that this was the problem. This was not enough for the Doctor who then went on to ask Poochie, who was playing Mum for the day, how she knew it was scoliosis. She also replied that it had been diagnosed as thus by a previous doctor. After five minutes of this back and forth banter, which led to an understanding of why we had to wait so long to see him, he finally had a look for himself. He decided that it was scoliosis, which of course we already knew. He then began to give a horrifying account of what treatment might be needed next by addressing myself and Poochie with "This won't scare you, but it will probably terrify him..." He opened his drawer and proceeded to pull out a bolt, and in front of Jay explained that he would need twenty or so of them inserted into his spine. For added effect he twisted the nuts at the end of each sentence. Jay is nineteen years old, has never been to hospital, has rarely been to the city and is a polite, pleasant, and sensible country boy. The doctor then went on to suggest that it was not always a successful operation. Poochie wanted to know how much the operation might cost. The Doctor was unwilling to discuss the subject which I considered strange given that he had supposedly performed this operation several times and would therefore have a good handle on the price. Instead, he sent us for an X-ray, across town, in rush hour, and asked us to return once it had been completed. By this time, Pops and Buzzy were becoming increasingly vexed at this huge wait and were not best pleased on hearing about the next two trips we had to make. Buzzy shot us across town and for once we were pleased with his reckless approach to driving because we just made it to the X-ray department, half an hour before they closed at 7 p.m. They were at least efficient and by closing time we had exited the Department with the pictures, having forked out $5,000 JMD (£25GBP/$30US) for them. We then returned to the doctors (far quicker given that the traffic was now easing) and were barely glanced at by the secretary who was by now far more preoccupied by her visiting husband and son.

The Doctor took the X-rays from us and put them on his fluorescent whiteboard.

"Hmmmm, it is severely damaged" he uttered sagely.

He then explained that we would not be able to work out the angle of the curve in the spine, whereas he, with his years of training would be far better qualified. He then produced from his desk a protractor, not unlike the ones eleven-year-old kids use in Mathematics classes and used it to work out the angle. He explained what would happen if the problem got worse and explained that if the operation was not a success Jay would not be able to stand up but would instead just fall over. Jay looked shell-shocked. The cost of the operation was brought up again. The doctor again refused to enter into that conversation which was frustrating because Poochie needed to know how much cash the family might need to rustle up. On being pressed the doctor told us we would have to ask his secretary and ushered us out of his room. Adolf said she would email the details because she would need to find out the cost of the screws and she said that even then she could not come up with a figure because it was dependent on the length of stay in the hospital. She could/would not even give us a ballpark figure. Poochie then forked out a further $5000JA for the privilege of the day's stress without being any further on in discovering how to go about the operation. This service is an example of private health in Jamaica. People pay for this. It should make those who criticise the brilliant National Health Service in the UK ashamed of themselves. We had been on the road for two hours to get to Kingston and had spent seven and a half hours getting to the position we were now in, which was practically the same as when we had left this morning. Everyone was tired and fed up except for Jay who was both those things as well as confused, scared and shocked. I felt cheated and I was not even the victim. My experience of the Health Service in Jamaica was not good. The Jamaican Government rakes in huge dollops of money from the tourist industry and I am really beginning to wonder where it goes. It certainly does not seem to filter down to those who need it most. When we got in the car to leave Kingston it was dark. Nobody in the car had wanted to even be in Kingston when it was dark, never mind try to find their way out. The daylight hustle and bustle that I had found so exhilarating, so much so that I was behaving like Dorothy when she first lands in Oz, had made way for activities and an atmosphere that was more reminiscent of a modern-day Sodom and Gomorrah. Everyone seemed to be either getting drunk or already there; scantily clad young women were shrugging off the lecherous calls of dirty old men, side-corner arguments were roaring and there was a heavy, heavy police presence, and there we were, stuck right in the middle of it. As we turned a corner, Pops asked me,

"Did you see that?"

I hadn't seen anything particularly notable in the direction he was pointing me, except for a cluster of armed and bullet proof vested officers.

It was explained to me.

There had been a murder.

I looked back. I initially did not believe that was why the cops were there because everyone else seemed to just be going about their business oblivious to the drama just two feet away from them. They were just walking on by, almost stepping over a prostrate body without breaking stride or gaze.

Kingston has become synonymous with violent gun crime, (as of August that year there had been 926 murders in the capital) but the attitude of Kingstonians is shockingly blasé. We had only moved a mile or so from the murder scene when flashing lights and sirens overwhelmed the car. We all looked at each other, none of us asking "Do they want us?" After Buzzy pulled over it became obvious that it was 'us' they were after as their car sidled up behind us. It was like the scene at the beginning of 'Mississippi Burning' and my heart sunk.

"COME OUT OF YOUR CAR WITH HANDS IN THE AIR!"

Buzzy slowly opened his door, and then realising he had his mobile phone attached to his wrist quickly shook it and the phone fell into his seat. He then slowly got out, arms in the air, walking towards the dazzling lights behind us. I stuck my head out of the window and could see a huge officer standing a respectful distance away from our car pointing his gun at us. He repeated that it was just the driver that they wanted but I kept my head out of the window, visible as a passenger. I figured that the presence of a white face might smooth things over, because if Buzzy was a criminal or murderer he would be highly unlikely to choose me as an accomplice in his misdemeanour; a clueless, easily identifiable and highly conspicuous white man. Lots of possible helpful solutions to the situation were racing through my mind. I thought I could tell them that I was a freelance journalist from the UK and that if they roughed up Buzzy in any way I would make sure that it made the papers across the globe. Then I came up with a better idea. Whilst at Reggae Sumfest, Chris Goldfinger, the BBC radio presenter had given me his card and I had it on my person. I figured that if asked, I would present this card pretending to be Chris Goldfinger, and those three letters 'BBC' would be our passport to freedom. Buzzy was being interrogated by another giant of a policeman who wore a bullet-proof vest and cradled a huge gun in his arms. After a relatively long chat, and much to our relief, he was finally allowed to return to the car. It had been a spot check, for what, we don't know. Buzzy later explained that had he left the car with the phone in his hand, the police might well have considered him armed and in Kingston they tend to shoot first and ask questions later.

Throughout the day I had become increasingly frustrated at not being able to get out of the car and just go for a wander, but now I was beginning to see the wisdom in my family not allowing it. Whilst all this was happening to us, passing civilians paid no interest and did not even look in our direction. The event had caused some excitement in our car though and there was a lot of chat about it and laughter on the way home. The drive back was long and arduous. Kingston to Pleasanton is mostly a single carriageway journey and we were held up several times by trucks choking on their own fumes. However, with the lights of houses in the distance, the journey was a visual treat. The hills seemed full of twinkling stars, and occasionally barely visible shapes could be made out on the porches, dispassionately watching the world go by. There was an interview with Beenie Man on the radio and he was discussing the Sumfest controversy. He seemed gracious regarding Bounty Killer and the whole 'fish' incident. On our return I discovered that Momma had been busy organising a 'surprise' for me. I badgered and pestered for a clue as to what my surprise might be, but it was to no avail. I was told that I would have to wait until the following day, but at least I knew my surprise would soon come and unlike today's surprise, I presumed it wouldn't be at the other end of an assault rifle.

Chapter Eighteen

The Jamaican Grand Prix

St Elizabeth is in South Central Jamaica and it is where a few of Momma's extended family now live. In Pleasanton Momma and family live relatively good lives; they have a nice house situated in a lovely town and they have a working vehicle despite Radar and co.'s attempts to make it less so. Momma's relatives however have not been so lucky. Momma wanted to show me how other members of the family live to illustrate further how less fortunate Jamaicans lead their daily lives. St Elizabeth is also where Momma's sister resides, Aunt Rose. Rose had been staying with us for the past five days and she had injected a new sense of liveliness and fun into the proceedings. Rose is older than Momma and I was surprised to occasionally hear her humorously threaten to "lick" Momma "in the head" when they were disagreeing on a point, something no-one else would even dare to think of doing. You can tell that her and Momma are from the same stock. Both are friendly, neither take any nonsense, and both have a laugh that positively bellows out. She is also a serial hugger and nearly every time I said something it was met with a request for a hug from Rose.

The journey would be longer than the trip to St. Thomas and therefore hard work for the drivers, and this was when my surprise revealed itself. My family had decided that Isaac would be one of the named drivers today. I was thrilled!

After three weeks of studying the psyche of your average Jamaican driver, I felt well prepared and was confident that I could handle all that the roads could throw at me. That was until I saw the hire car. Actually, I heard it first, squeaking and blowing like it had emphysema as it trundled up the hill to

Momma's the night before. I had taken it for a brief spin up to the closest Jerk Pork vendor two minutes away, and was somewhat disconcerted by the number of lights that illuminated the dashboard. It appeared that nothing worked properly on this shadow of a vehicle. When I touched the brakes, they made a sound like an injured animal and this being Jamaica, I half wondered if one might still be lodged underneath. They were spongy and even with the pedal floored the car seemed to make little effort to try and stop. This should have worried me, but instead I was rather excited. That night I prepared for my journey by writing down what I considered were the most important things to remember in a sort of crash (perhaps not the best word to use here) course in Jamaican Highway Rules.

THE SIX RULES OF JAMAICAN DRIVING

1) Drive as fast as possible. You are the King of the road. All animals and pedestrians are secondary to your safety and should any get in your way, don't be afraid to hit them.

2) Indicators are entirely optional. Try not to use them unless a police officer is in the vicinity.

3) Never wait. If a car is in your way or pausing to turn at a junction; try to overtake it, undertake it, or simply leave centimetres to spare as you swerve to avoid it.

4) Potholes are more important than oncoming traffic. You need to ensure that you spend as much time on the wrong side of the road avoiding them as on the correct side, and never let oncoming traffic put you off in your mission to protect your own vehicle.

5) When approaching a corner, never, ever slow down. Honk your horn loudly so they know you are coming. If there's an accident, it's their fault. You told them you were coming.

6) Finally, and perhaps most importantly, you must drive in the full knowledge that the driver approaching your vehicle at some speed and on the same side of the road is more of a rotten coward than you are.

We were taking two cars today with me at the wheel of the hired death trap and Buzzy taking the controls of the trustier vehicle that was Pop's. I was to follow the lead car and having seen Buzzy drive, I knew that this would be an extreme challenge. The first major problem I encountered was to do with the indicators. They were on the opposite side to the car I normally drive and likewise the windscreen wipers. Consequently, the first few junctions I encountered were accompanied by the 'nails down the blackboard' screech of the blasted blades much to the irritation of my cargo of Snoop, TJ, Kaydee and Poochie. We began by heading on the road to Kingston at an initially sedate pace, so I was able to fully appreciate the early morning clouds cutting through the mountains. However, after Buzzy had entered a tunnel honking his horn loudly (as most Jamaicans do) he seemed to get excited and forget that he was playing Rain Man to me. Now I was in the Jamaican Grand Prix, which is like most other Grand Prix except the fatal bends have not been smoothed out. My apprenticeship was over just five minutes after it had begun, as Buzzy began tearing down the busy two-way traffic taking the racing line at every heart-stopping corner and driving totally and utterly on his brakes. However, after fifteen minutes of complete horror trying to keep up with him, the safety car came out in the shape of a truck wedged on the side of the road, which on this bend, was also the middle of the road. I was relieved. Almost immediately though, the stuck truck unfortunately became unstuck, the flags were down, and the race was back on. Every bend was being negotiated with almost a complete turn of the wheel. I was following the racing line now, which was almost completely on the wrong side of the circuit. Potholes were being miraculously skirted as I found my eyes looking ahead, then at the potholes, ahead, potholes, ahead, potholes. As we raced along this by now familiar journey, I knew I was in the proximity of the vagina rock, but also knew that finding it would just have to wait because I was putting such fierce concentration into my driving. Sweat was cascading down my face and I was smoking constantly. Buzzy finished the first segment of the race by a good distance from the 'rookie' Isaac. Flat Bridge was the cause for a new delay. I reflected on our race which incidentally had not been ours alone. Oh no, our competition was frequently interrupted by other Hari Kiri devotees tearing inside and outside of us recklessly. Philosopher Jean Paul Sartre claimed that 'Hell was other people', Isaac Hye claims that 'Hell is other Jamaican drivers'. I had begun to understand why Jamaica has yet to produce a successful Formula One contender; it is simply because not one of them can drive in straight line. Flat Bridge looked wonderful again today, but several times now there have been snarl ups because as mentioned, the bridge is a hazardous, tight, single lane, with a drop and water on both sides. There are traffic lights, and even though these are mostly ignored, even Buzzy couldn't overtake on this stretch. I hoped the pause in the proceedings would help remind him of his duty.

Not a bit of it.

Once we were over the bridge it was every man for himself again. Cars swarmed over each other, sometimes overtaking when there was no space to overtake by simply muscling in and forcing the sandwiching cars aside. I had begun to get the hang of things a little and began throwing the car and my passengers around in wild abandon just in order to keep on the bumper of Buzzy. In fact, I was beginning to love it! Then Buzzy went to overtake a truck with another truck approaching in the distance. I followed suit, to a horrified scream from the passenger seats of,

"Noooooooooooo!"

I simply muttered "Yes!", gritted my teeth and determinedly slammed my foot to the floor but I had forgotten I was driving an automatic and so, despite pumping furiously on the accelerator, there was no response. My mind was thinking "Oops, I've misjudged this one" as the truck careered towards us. I began pumping again and again, then with an audible clunk, it miraculously stirred into action. I was leant over the steering wheel as if this would give me added momentum, swaying back and forth like a child on a swing. The gap began to appear; a quarter of a car space, a third of a car space, a half of a car space. As three quarters of a car space appeared I thought "Fuck it, I've got to go for it NOW", so I plunged the car over to the left, missing the front of the truck I was trying to overtake, and the one I was trying to avoid, by a matter of inches. The car was silent. The truck behind me wasn't though, and he was letting me know what a close shave I'd had via his horn and his hand gestures. Unfortunately, Buzzy appeared not to have seen the drama unfold behind him, as he was chasing down the next poor sap to put through hell and so I had no choice but to continue chasing Buzzy having not fully recovered from a near heart attack and having not heard a word from my petrified passengers. The Jamaican roads are littered with advertising slogans or driving cautions. Most of the signs today were simply a blur, but one did catch my eye. It was along the lines of 'If you Overtake, you might meet the Undertaker'. By now I was matching Buzzy pothole swerve for pothole swerve, and instead of instantly following his overtaking manoeuvres, I waited for the opportunity to make my own and was soon catching up to him although to be fair, he did wait for me on a couple of occasions. The adrenaline rush was brought to a temporary halt when we made a halfway stop at a Juici Patties. I reckoned I had now completed an inventory of all their branches on the island and I thought that was worthy of at least a certificate or something.

As we all bundled out of our two cars there was much laughing and whooping from the lead vehicle. But Momma looked at me seriously and began to talk to the others in impenetrable patois once more. I was either being threatened with being shot, possibly for putting four of her family in absolute danger, or the term 'Shotta' means something else.

Buzzy explained that it in fact means a 'bad man', and in this context it meant a 'bad man driver', as in I was bossing the road.

Respec'! The passengers in the other car were impressed by my ability on the Jamaican Roads of Death. My passengers however did not seem quite as thrilled as I was with my newly bestowed title. Momma then looked at the dream machine I was proudly sat in, engine still running.

"What are those lights?" she asked quizzically whilst gesturing at the dashboard.

Not being even vaguely interested in cars other than the requirements that it has a stereo and can get me from A to B I replied,

"I don't know. There is one with a line thingy on it, one that looks like a deformed light bulb, and the other says ABS".

She began tut-tutting and asked me to turn off the engine, turn it back on, and have a little drive around the car park. It was then she heard the brakes. She went ballistic, demanding to know from where the car had been hired and saying that it

St Elizabeth livestock

would have to go back the minute we arrived home in Pleasanton. I pleaded for my new girlfriend who I had decided to christen *Gladys* to stay, but she was adamant that it would have to go back. Rose came over, asked me for a hug and said that she was with me regarding the car. It must stay. Drinks out of a cool box in the car park, a tasty patty, and we were back on the roads. With my 'Shotta' title newly won, I was not about to relinquish it so soon and I wanted to prove that Gladys was worthy of staying with me. I matched Buzzy in the arena of lethal driving all the way through the parishes of St. Ann, St. Catherine, Clarendon, Manchester, and St. Elizabeth. By the time we reached our destination I felt like I had speed pulsing through my veins and was saddened that I would not be getting another 'hit' for a few hours. Our final road had been barely a road, it being rutted with stones and grass and the roots of trees. It led up to Momma's momma's house, which was barely a house. It measured the size of an average living room. The wood was cracked and peeling, and the metal roof had holes riddled through it. Once inside, huge beams of light shot through the dark so radiantly that I though the house had electricity. It was the sunlight coming through the various gaps in the walls. This was another example of the Jamaica you don't find in the tourist brochures or inside the luxury of the gated communities. We chatted with Momma's bed-ridden momma for twenty minutes or so. She had moved to St. Elizabeth to be nearer the majority of her family. Her house was neat and tidy and there was a panoply of animals in the environs. There were chickens; pigs, goats, cats, dogs, and the most enormous bull I have ever seen in my life. This might seem idyllic to some, but perhaps only those who have a choice whether to live like that or not. The reality for most is Hobbes-ian; nasty, brutal, and short, and I sensed that the old lady before me was living her final days, weeks, at most a year. After saying our goodbyes, we went on a whistle-stop tour of family. Nearly all lived in similar conditions. This was hard, country life. Towards the end we were exhausted having seen six sets of cousins, uncles, aunties, sisters, people who they were on nodding terms with on the road, the postman, his dog...rae rae.

Our final stop was at a cousin's who had lived in Birmingham in the UK for a while. I joked with him that he was lucky not to have picked up the accent to which he chuckled. He had laid on a fantastic spread of food which I could unfortunately not partake of having something of an upset stomach, most probably driving related. It was here that we also said goodbye to Aunt Rose which was a shame because she had been such a lively and fun presence in her time with us. But now it was action stations again. Buzzy revved, I revved, we exchanged glances, and then we were off. We tore down the country roads like we were on a four-lane motorway with no other traffic in sight. We zipped through rainforests and zapped through villages whilst overtaking, undertaking and generally driving with no concern for our own personal safety; or for that of our passengers. A deluge of rain stopped us in our tracks, and it came down when we were in, would you believe it, Manchester, the U.K. equivalent being synonymous with rain. To be precise we were in Mandeville in Manchester, which is delightfully pretty and is the upper-class town of the Parish. We skirted it rather than going through it but it looked picturesque and I now wished I was not in this vehicular fight for honour with Buzzy so that I could potentially have made a little detour. We passed through Santa Cruz whilst still being pestered by rain. The slower pace gave me a chance to take in the surroundings. It looked like a very busy market town on a very busy market day. People were crossing the road in all sorts of different directions, weaving and sliding, shouting and bawling, laughing and living. Santa Cruz was all pastel shades and prettiness making it a bright and aesthetically pleasing little place. This could have been considered a pit stop because we were soon flying through the country lanes again. After we had skirted Spanish Town it was back into the chicanes and hairpin bends on the steep climb into Pleasanton. Once we had arrived home, and under Momma's instructions, I sadly made my way to the car rental garage. It looked like Gladys would be forcibly taken from me. However, after a quick check underneath and some twiddling and fiddling, Gladys was back with me, squeak free but still lit up like the Aurora Bourialis. The mechanic convinced Momma that she was now road worthy and I was thrilled to know that I had her for another day! I celebrated with some Jerk Chicken and a small bottle of the vicious spirit that passes for rum here, Wray and Nephew. It had been quite an adventure today. As the cars were unpacked it was clear that we were returning with enough gifted fruit and vegetables to open our own store. There were five melons, a whopping pumpkin, sour sap, sweet sap, Ackee, ginger, and guinep. I knew that tomorrow we would eat like kings. All of this had been given to us by the various relatives whom we had encountered along the way. It is their currency, and yet their generosity is moving.

After the excitement and vicarious thrills of brutal Kingston, it had been a relief to return to the real country once more, where the people have kind-hearted spirits. Everywhere we have been we have been offered food, both to eat on the spot and in the form of a take-away. These people *are* Jamaica, and once again I return to my mantra that it would only be fair if they were rewarded for their contributions to this wonderful country in the form of further help from the powers that be, both home and abroad.

Chapter Nineteen

I Don't Want A Holiday In The Sun

As a result of my driving skills and the kudos I gained from that mad and unstable trip to St. Elizabeth it seemed that I was now fully accepted, in family circles at least, as "a real Jamaican". Since I had the pleasure of Gladys's company for another day, I decided to take her on a jaunt down to Ocho Rios. This was my maiden solo voyage, and I was chuffed! I had not yet bought the customary souvenirs for loved ones back home and my money was dwindling away. I told myself that I would not need to race because I was not following Buzzy but the minute I got behind that wheel a sense of machismo overtook me - "mi senses dem get hot" - and I immediately began flying round corners that never seem to end and careering through villages at breakneck speed. I was brought to a natural standstill by Fern Gully which requires stealth and care so as to avoid the huge craters in the road, and once done, the descent into Ochi is a sunny breeze. I parked up and took in my surroundings. Ochi has parts of town that are tourist havens and even though I had hoped to avoid these Babylonian hotspots, I realised that I would simply have to brace myself and be a proper tourist for today. As I began walking along the street, I saw the first of a plentiful number of craft markets and perched on the corner was the Reggae Mix stall. It was manned by a striking looking Rasta who has the kindest face and eyes you could ever hope to encounter. I was looking for some of the latest music to take home with me, and my new friend had it in abundance.

I then moved deeper into the market and braced myself knowing that what was about to happen was a necessary evil in order to track down presents; I knew because it had happened to me in Turkey, Israel, Spain and many other places I have previously visited. However, the market stall vendors here are desperate for business and they put their fellow stall owners in any bazaar around the globe to shame. They pounce on you, paw at you and make you want to flee immediately. It is a highly stressful experience given that everybody in the market wants a piece of you and won't take any amount of elaborate explanation as a suitable excuse for you not examining their wares. And the thing is, every stall in Ochi looks the same. They all sell the same wood carvings, paintings, Bob-bilia, trinkets, and charms as each other which means that you experience a feeling of déjà vu before you can appease them with a purchase of some sort and make a relieved exit. As the next stall is entered the chorus goes up from neighbouring stalls demanding that you visit them. If you forget, you are implored with tearful eyes and praying hands before guiltily agreeing to enter and have things shoved in your face and up your nose and any other available oriface. Nearly every vendor explains that you can look around their shop for free, thereby suggesting that you are about to encounter an utterly unique experience which you really should be paying for whereas in fact it houses the same sights you had encountered just two minutes before in the previous stall. They also claim that there is no pressure to buy, before virtually tearing your limbs off and pleading so persuasively that you feel inclined to purchase more of the same just to get them to leave you alone. Some people can handle this type of experience with consummate ease, but for me it was a traumatic experience and after an hour so of being the dutiful tourist I began to get entirely fed up and both my demeanour and my tone took on a new aggression. As such I was not bothered by them nearly as much and managed to leave with a modest bag of better goodies. I wandered around a few

Western looking shops in the town which had everything priced in American Dollars, and everything was priced for the bearers of those dollars, i.e., extremely high. I went to grab something to eat and was disappointed to discover that I had missed breakfast, so instead sat down to the regular ital veg, rice and peas. After further meanderings in the mid-day sun, I needed to cool down. I had placed a towel and a pair of shorts inside Gladys's 'batty' in case I fancied a dip, and so returned to my beau before hitting the beach.

I was going to the beach to swim. I have never been great at lazing around doing nothing and struggle with the notion of lying in the sun when I could be doing more interesting things. As I passed the numerous gated hotels that spill onto the sand I admired the vast stretch awaiting my imprint. This was not a public beach like the one I had enjoyed so much at Priory, but a private beach that you had to pay to use. It reminded me of a visit to a U.S. Native American reservation near Niagara a few years back. I had stopped at a diner and there was a framed story on the wall. It told of white settlers trying to buy land from the true American inhabitants, in this case the Susquamish tribe whose Chief Seattle responded with philosophical wisdom explaining that he could not sell the land because it did not belong to him but to a Higher Power. This was not good enough for the good ol' English boys who responded by taking it by brute force, murder, and pillage.

The point I am trying to make is that the sea and the sand surely belong to everyone.

I grudgingly paid my $200 JA and darted through the gate, with my towel tucked under my arm like a child heading to the local pool. The beach was populated with predominantly white people, by far the highest concentration I had seen thus far, all of whom seemed to be sitting around doing nothing. At

Priory everyone had been either swimming, playing football or having loud raucous fun, but here the beach resembled the type you encounter in the south of Spain, with jet skis taking precedence over swimmers, and screaming brat kids deafening the neighbouring fondling couples. The space in which to swim was minimal due to a line of buoys guarding the entry to the vastness of the ocean in which the jet skis functioned. At the deepest point of my allotted swimming space, I could still stand up and the water barely tickled my chest and I am only 5'10. The swim-able stretch was approximately the width of an average pool, and so after flailing up and down it a couple of times, I was cool but irritated that I could not go deeper into the crystal seas. I had a quick wash off, changed back into my clothes, and disappointedly headed back to Gladys. I stopped at Mother's for a veggie patty but on pulling out of Ochi, I realised that I did not know where the hell I was going. I knew I had to take a left by the Shell petrol station but could only find an Esso.

Then my phone rang.

It was Michael the mechanic. He had been driving out of Ochi and had seen me heading off in totally the wrong direction towards the parish of St. Mary. He had phoned to alert me to my error which I unconvincingly blustered off (I am a 'real Jamaican' now lest you forget so I can't be seen to be getting lost) as me just having a drive around Ochi before I headed home. I must have circumnavigated the town fifteen times before the Shell garage, which was obviously very good at hiding, came into view. The drive back to Pleasanton was at least thrilling, most probably because I had decided that the green car that was occasionally right on my bumper would not be allowed to pass. It chased me through the Gully, where it occasionally pulled up alongside as we both navigated the holes, but every time it threatened to go past, I hammered the accelerator. I roared into Pleasanton with my pride intact and sweat swimming down me, seconds ahead of the loser in the green demon. When I got home, I began to think about Michael's phone call. My family are very protective and worry when I head out on foot into the village on my own. I wondered if they had ensured that my first 'solo' trip, and especially my first 'solo' trip in a car, was not entirely 'solo'. Maybe Michael was around simply to check I was doing fine. Or maybe its paranoia induced by the humungous amount of weed I have ingested on the trip. I was keen to get some proper food down me and now that DeeDee is back with her lovable brood it would mean that the house and 'mi belly' would be full. And so, when I skipped down into the kitchen that evening it was full of wonderful food, laughter, and love, in fierce opposition to the sterile and unfulfilling time I had today as a normal tourist. I love this family and tonight they were helping to assuage the pangs of loss over the departure of my Gladys.

Chapter Twenty

Emancipation Day - Poochie's Birthday!

August 1st is Emancipation Day in Jamaica, a national holiday. I woke up early to discover that I only had one cigarette which I smoked almost instantly despite trying to resist the urge knowing that I would then have to go out on the Great Cigarette Hunt this morning. Buying cigarettes in Jamaica is a trial. It shouldn't be because everybody seems to smoke. But there are several shops I have visited that look like they should sell cigarettes, but don't. This morning, being unable to resist the cravings any longer, I determined to find some. I walked out of the sleeping house and hiked to the first shop in the village. I say shop, but it is essentially a house attached to a beautifully crafted, colour laden garden, with a room the size of a lavatory acting as the business premises. The keeper, once I had roused him, didn't have any smokes but he could sense the frenzied panic I was in and so directed me up the hill to a blue house and told me to shout them and they would be able to sate my desires. I followed his suggestion, by now resembling a marathon runner at the halfway stage, caked in sweat and with blowing cheeks. I had been sent to a house, not a shop, and so I shouted to the man who was hacking through his garden foliage with a huge machete and asked if he sold cigarettes. He ceased his lethal blade work and asked how many I wanted. "Two packs" I replied.

"I don't sell them in packs" he responded.

It is a Jamaican 'ting' that a lot of vendors sell singles and not packs. It was 9 o'clock in the morning. Two or three were not going to last me all day and I wasn't sure where else would be open given that it was Emancipation Day. I toyed with the idea of asking for nineteen, but he was holding a machete.

There was one more shop to visit, a garden shed with a hatch, before I self-combusted. I was soaked through with sweat by now and it was just approaching ten minutes past nine in the morning. I knew that this shop stocked what I was after, and I was cursing the fact that I had not headed straight to it but in this heat the temptation is to take short cuts. I picked up two packs and a breakfast bun.

As I headed back home, chain smoking every step of the way, I pondered on the importance of this Bank Holiday. Emancipation Day is a celebration of the release of Jamaica's slaves from bondage and as such it holds a special place in the hearts of Jamaicans. However, of far more historical weight and gravitas to her, is the fact that August 1st is Poochie's birthday. When I got back all hands were on deck preparing for this momentous occasion. Buzzy, Radar and their young friend Titus were in the backyard and already cooking bounteous amounts of chicken and pork, whilst a strange looking soup was slowly bubbling on the home-made fire. Radar was also in charge of the sounds and was accompanying the tunes even more lustily than normal. The alcohol had arrived in crates the evening before, and so everything was prepared for the birthday girl. She eventually made her entrance, sashaying down the stairs in an outfit of immaculately matched patriotic threads, all greens, yellows and blacks. This was a holiday, but Snoop had decided to pull his hair apart the day before which meant that we reluctantly ventured out to see if the stylists was open. Pops, having heard of my driving exploits wanted to witness it for himself in his car. He was lucky because I did not have my glasses with me, so I had to travel at a sedate pace just to see the blurred and barely perceptible potholes out of my weak and overworked eyes. I dropped the hairdressing party off before Pops and I headed to Keith's to pick up some callaloo from his stunning garden and true to form we were also given eggs and bananas. Every tree in the garden bears food of some variety and it was in the shadow of this setting that we began to talk about Jamaica and Emancipation. We reflected on my trip to pay my respects to Paul Bogle, Marcus Garvey, and Alexander Bustamante, and I wondered aloud why Bob Marley is not yet in the pantheon of National Heroes. Keith, who knew Bob personally claimed that it was because Bob would not have died for his country, as two of the three had. He went on to big up Bob for his success in spreading Reggae music and the Rasta faith, but he was realistic about the type of man Bob was. Several Jamaicans I have spoken to since my arrival seem to feel that Bob sold Peter Tosh and Bunny Wailer down the river, and that Bob was not absolved from a bit of, in Keith's words "fuck'ry". Bob is more of a thorny issue in Jamaica than abroad. There is much criticism of the way his legacy has been handled and of the attached rampant commercialism that his family seem to have indulged in through using the Marley name. Nevertheless, nearly every Jamaican I have met has asked if I have been to Nine Mile yet. He is still someone of whom Jamaicans are rightly proud of.

We continued to shoot the breeze, the subject turning to mosquitoes. I was asking Keith if these annoying and vicious little insects had any useful purpose. Bees stings but they create honey yet these blighters who at times caused me severe itching issues seem to offer no positive contribution to the world whatsoever. Keith's take on them was philosophical. He suggested that their use was to "kill off the wicked", a typical Jamaican explanation then, and I was reassured that he wasn't referring to me. At this point in the conversation the phone call came to inform Pops and I that the hairdressing party were now ready for pick up, so we left Keith with an invite for later and I once more gave Pops the impression that the evil driving of which he had heard so much could not have been achieved by the squinting and hunched body next to him. Driving through Moneague we passed one of my regular supermarkets which was closed (as was nearly everywhere else) so it seemed that even the wonderfully named proprietor of that establishment who I had not yet met, Squeeze-Eye, was having the day off too. Since I have been here, Squeeze-Eye has been referred to as Squeeze-Head, Popeye and a few other monikers all suggesting some sort of physical deformity. I dread to think what Squeeze-Eye really looks like.

When we arrived back in Pleasanton, the soup was already being consumed and the first dents in the alcohol had been made. I was offered some soup. I like soup, but soup in Jamaica can contain some nasty surprises. I wanted to know that my cup did not contain any neck, testicles, or tails before I agreed to give it a go. "It's just chicken soup" I was firmly told by a reveller. Ital out of the window, once more out of politeness, I began to sup it hesitantly and discovered that it had a lovely taste. As I became more confident that this was basic chicken soup I took bigger and less focused gulps until a menacing sight rose, scaly and Jaws-like from the depths and up to the top of the broth. It was a chicken toe! I gagged and spat out all that was in my mouth and threw my cup down much to the merriment of all those within my vicinity. What a rotten trick to play on an unsuspecting lapsed vegetarian. That's it, no more meat even if the provider might be offended! Guests arrived at the party all day including Keith, who surprised me by turning up in a swish get up in contrast to his usual dishevelled gardening clothes. Mr. Hedges and family from the Bensonton drive also appeared. No-one brought gifts or cards for the birthday girl, and Poochie did not even know half of the revellers who were simply friends of other invitees. This is the 'norm' in Jamaica. It also seemed that Poochie's reward for being 21 again (ahem) was to wait hand and foot on the guests along with Momma. I was introduced to most of the party goers whose names and nicknames are so exotic that I had a job remembering them. A couple I was introduced to were variously described as husband and wife, fiancées, and partners. When I asked someone for the specific detail of their matrimonial relationship, I was told "Mi nuh know".

As with the names of people in this most laid-back of countries, there is a lack of precision in the descriptions of relationships, jobs, and numbers of children. Even at the football match in Claremont no-one seemed to know much about who was playing and how long the games were. It seems that anything and everything that you are told in Jamaica should be taken with a pinch of salt because there is a real looseness about such conventions, and it really is far too much effort to be absolutely accurate. As if to emphasise this point, one of the guests had been telling me about a triple murder that had taken place in a big house on the outskirts of Pleasanton 'the other day'. But nearly every story he told began with 'The other day' despite it being apparent that some of the events obviously took place years ago. It's another Jamaica thing. The party had begun at midday, and it ambled amiably through the afternoon and into the evening. There came a point in the early dusk when the alcohol and the weed I had ingested fused into a beautiful intoxicating anaesthetic, and I just felt overwhelmingly blessed and blissed out. Everything was Irie. Food, drink, and weed had been in constant supply throughout the day and of course it would have been rude to have turned down any of them, whether they contained toes or not.

Buzzy and his friends left as darkness descended having witnessed the cake cutting which had been accompanied by a prayer from the local preacher. I thought the prayer had finished on several occasions, but the preacher was still finding people to bless after almost five minutes. The boys had gone to find an Emancipation Day dance and had invited me to join them, but by this time, having had a liquid diet of Red Stripe, Guinness, Baileys and 60% rum, and having lost control of my arms, legs, and mouth; bed was my destination for the rest of the evening. I fell asleep ruminating on the emancipation of Jamaica's slaves. When people in the 'developed' world think of the abolition of slavery they think of William Wilberforce and the supposed altruism of the men that led the campaign to rid the world of the savagery and suffering caused by the slave trade. However, I am learned in this field and as I had intimated to Herpaul Lincoln whilst in Morant Bay, the history books have been too kind to a lot of the abolitionists, many of whom had sugar interests elsewhere, Spain for instance, and therefore it was in their economic interest to put an end to slavery. Most of the real heroes of emancipation and of the abolition of slavery were in Jamaica itself; Nanny of the Maroons, who fought using military tactics against the English until she died at their hands in the 1750's and who, according to legend used her batty (backside) to return the enemies' bullets, Sam Sharpe, a preacher of high intelligence and principle, who did much to educate slaves and then led the strategically planned and island wide 1831 Christmas Rebellion, and of course the magnificent Paul Bogle. It should not be forgotten that resistance can take many forms, and during slavery simple acts such as 'tool breaking' could be very costly for the slave owners and so seemingly small measures undertaken by slaves can also be viewed as an unheralded manifestation of rebellion that further contributed to the eradication of such a cruel practice. These were the real heroes of slavery. The picture painted of the abolitionists as beacons of 'fair play 'is more fitting of Dali than Constable. Marxist philosophers have suggested that no society develops into another society (e.g., feudalism to capitalism) until its previous society has exhausted itself. Slavery had served its purpose, was becoming expensive and was moving beyond its usefulness and there were rich pickings to be made elsewhere. It would not have been ditched otherwise. So for me the real heroes of abolition were those who fought brutality from within. But you know what it is like in our black sheep, black mark, blackmail, pure as snow, whiter than white, culture. The good guy is always white, and even better if he can be American or English too. The evening 'erb leads to heavy thoughts.

Chapter Twenty-One

Nine Mile

Music has been my life, and my initial interest in Jamaica was sparked by a man who bestrode the world preaching messages of love and unity through his sometimes sweet and sometimes coruscating songs. Describing him as simply a man is possibly an injustice given the way he is revered by some in Jamaica and many across the globe, but that is how he described himself; "just a man". Bob Marley was one of several musicians who conspired to alert me to the enigma that is Jamaica. This small in stature but great lion of a man who performed with incredible passion and intensity, served up songs imbued with the mysteries of his Rastafarian faith shimmering through them and I was hooked. Long after his life had been so tragically curtailed his musical spirit remains, and I was still discovering some of his lesser-known works sometime after he had joined his beloved JAH. For someone who had previously been fed on the spiritually shallow foci of the capitalist West, I felt that Bob Marley meant it, man. He sang for the downtrodden of the world and strived to get people to pull together in the hope that they wouldn't suffer on the scale that they did whilst he was alive, and sadly still do. He also put his money where his mouth was gifting much of his fortune to those local Jamaicans who needed dire help. And then he died; a victim of the life lottery known as cancer. Like an earlier star, he packed in an incredible amount of living into thirty something years of life and Bob, along with his predecessor, a carpenter by trade, has left a legacy that has seen him revered as a sainted hero standing on the pedestal of love and peace. I still remember exactly where I was when the mournful strains of *No Woman No Cry* came on the radio signalling to the English speakingworld that Bob Marley, physically at least, was no more.

During the 1970's Reggae and Rastafari was difficult to ignore. In England it helped that bands I loved such as The Clash and Public Image Limited promoted the wonderful works of Jah that were being created halfway across the world. The Clash's intelligent words, passionate sound, and integrity appealed to me, and their enthusiastic championing of the likes of U-Roy, Dillinger, Junior Murvin, Lee 'Scratch' Perry and numerous others was hard to ignore. On Don Letts' magnificent 'Westway to the World' documentary you see that the band's love for reggae music was, and still is, raw. Paul Simonon's magnificent reggae inspired bass lines, Mick Jones's appreciation of the unique cover art of the genre, and Joe Strummer's hand on head Marley pose and his warm and comical stories of his visits to Jamaica attest to the band's affection for Jamaican music. Similarly, John Lydon of The Sex Pistols and Public Image Limited (PiL) fame, was also a big reggae fan and in 1978 he visited Jamaica and hung out with Dennis Brown and Big Youth amongst others. Lydon's knowledge of reggae from that era is encyclopaedic and in an interview with the L.A. Times in 2007 he declared:

"Reggae to me is not an affectation. I heard it growing up in the council flats (the U.K.'s low-cost government housing). It's a way of life, it's not entertainment. Now saying that, Jamaican music has been ruined by the American gangsta rap influence. There's a nastiness and bitterness in the music now. I don't think they know who the enemy is anymore".

Lydon's love of reggae is grounded in the authentic and revolutionary conscious branch of the genre and in reggae John obviously identified a similar rebellious spirit to punk and post-punk that you can hear in the attitude of both of his bands, in his lyrics and in Jah Wobble's bass heavy PiL lines. The variant of ska that emerged in the U.K., engineered by the musical genius of Jerry Dammers and spearheaded by his magical The Specials was the soundtrack to my youth and as such it pushed me into investigating the ska scene of sixties Jamaica which gave way to Reggae in the seventies, which in turn gave Bob Marley the platform upon which to spread his music and his message.

At the same time, I discovered *The Harder They Come* and *Rockers*, two Jamaican movies that are Robin Hood tales of the downtrodden overcoming the powers that be, in turn providing psychic relief to sufferahs of the island. Perry Henzell's *The Harder They Come* tells of a country boy coming to the big city of Kingston, and after initial trials and tribulations, morphing into a criminal on the run, much to the excitement of the local media and the people. It ends in a memorable shoot out on a beach between Ivan (played by Jimmy Cliff) and the police that is reminiscent of the Spaghetti Westerns that were beloved of Jamaicans in the 1970's. Indeed, the scene in the picture house where a cowboy movie is being shown is one of the most memorable in the film. Cliff's performance alongside the scorching soundtrack is equally memorable. What comes across as an entertaining work of fiction is based on the true story of Rhygin, an outlaw who died in a shootout with the police in 1948. Meanwhile Patrick Hulsey's *Rockers* is a homage to the Rastafarian community and is an open indictment of the Babylon 'shit-stem'. The opening scene of a Rasta community up in the hills performing Satta Massagana, partially in the Ethiopian language of Amharic, is simply mesmerising. The fact that the actors were all musicians, well known and not so well known, is remarkable given the stellar acting performances they give. With a cast including Gregory Isaacs, Jacob Miller, Burning

Spear, Dillinger, and Big Youth, it is no surprise that the soundtrack is a work of genius. The scene where Leroy 'Horsemouth' Wallace and Winston Rodney (Burning Spear) reason before Rodney sings accompanied only by the sea, is spellbinding. Spear's delivery of *Jah Nuh Dead* is untouchable as the most spiritual invocation to Jah captured in a movie. *Rockers* is a trickster tale for the twentieth century. Trickster tales were a form of psychic relief for slaves, in that they normally took the form of the underdog overwhelming the master. This might take the form of a fly deceiving a spider, or a mouse deceiving a cat. In this case, the underdogs gain a pyrrhic victory over Babylon. With such musical and celluloid baggage it would have been remiss of me not to pay my respects to Robert Nesta Marley whilst in Jamaica and so Nine Mile, the place in which he was born, was to be my next destination.

I decided in my own perverse fashion to lay off the weed for the visit to Bob Marley's birthplace in Nine Mile. It was to be the first day I had given it a rest since I got to Jamaica. It felt weird. I have ingested so much of the stuff that I am probably on a permanent high anyway. The attitude of various governments around the world towards marijuana/sensimilla seems to be total and utter confusion. In Jamaica it is now legal, and previously was tolerated to some extent, so long as it wasn't flaunted. In the UK marijuana had been a Category 'C' drug, then upgraded to Category 'B' only to be downgraded but now again stands as Category 'B', flying in the face of the governmental health agencies who have argued that it should remain exactly where it was in Category 'C'. There are far more lethal things in the world like cigarettes, alcohol, Jamaican drivers and my recent discovery, mosquitoes. In fact, it is interesting that governments always jump on any new and not yet fully developed evidence suggesting the effects of marijuana are harmful, which to me, seems to smack of desperation. They know that their policies are hypocritical, taxing three of the four perils mentioned above (can you tax mosquitoes?), and then outlawing a far less harmful substance. As I have said, the sensible thing, the legalising of marijuana, would be of great worth to millions of people across the globe for both recreational and medical purposes. It would also mean that the billions of dollars that Jamaica achieve through tourism each year (really, where does it go?) would be dwarfed by a far more lucrative cash crop.

We took the road to St. Ann's Bay before navigating a hairpin in Claremont and beginning the ascent through St. Ann's Parish. We passed a church which had its doors wide open allowing the mellifluous tambourines and choirs to provide a Gospel soundtrack as we moved through the town. It seemed apt because as well as being his birthplace, Nine Mile is also where Bob Marley is buried. The sun was fighting to come out but failing as the heavier clouds sought to dominate the day. We bumped into Mr. Hedges' family returning from church, and as is customary, we blocked the road to have a chat with them. Everyone walking the by-ways and almost highways of Jamaica today seemed to be dressed in their Sunday best, and I mean their best. Men and boys were in suits and ties with finely polished shoes pounding the rough roads to church. Young girls had time consuming coiffures framing their innocent faces, and the women looked smart and modest, many balancing their milliner's finest atop their exotic hairstyles. Church is still a serious business in Jamaica. They could have been heading to any of the numerous places of worship that line Claremont's picturesque roadways. The scenery became more incredible the higher we climbed, and I just know that when I leave Jamaica and return home, everything is going to look ugly and small.

I then saw the strangest sight. A man, with a doll the size of a five-year-old child cradled in his arms, was striding along the road with a steely look on his face. I thought my eyes were deceiving me, so I glanced back, and what I saw is as reported. No-one else seemed to have noticed this strange vision. Maybe it was weed withdrawal.

Pops suddenly slammed on the brakes to prevent us hurtling into a bunch of livestock that were spread out all over the road. As he tried to slowly manoeuvre through them, he muttered "You have to watch these" and is if to prove a point, a suicidal goat leapt straight in front of us. Pops also pointed out that the shepherd was constantly with his flock because if he left them, "somebody would tief dem". I had read several stories in the newspapers about court cases involving those guilty of goat stealing. As we rose higher still into the mountains the roads became more treacherous with sheer drops on either side, and we seemed to be hovering above the whole of the island. This part of the Parish of St. Ann looked utterly inaccessible, and I considered how it would be a struggle to get a message to Kingston from here, never mind spreading that message to the whole of the world. When Bob was traversing these roads as a yout' he would not have had the benefit of a motor car either.

Mind you, when Pops missed a virtually 180 degrees turn on the road, I quite fancied walking myself. Further still and Pops once more had to slam on his brakes to avoid a car coming in the opposite direction and as he did so he mounted a fragment of wall that sent my head crashing into the roof of the car. It looked like I would be arriving at Nine Miles battered and bruised. The car that had almost killed us had a banner across the front windscreen. In England this would most likely have announced the arrival of Kyle and Karen, but

Nine Miles from where? Who knows?

in Jamaica things are different. This banner proclaimed, "Good Over Evil", and I have seen similar prophecies on several cars, but this seemed apt today given that I was travelling to the home of a man who used holy books to spread such positive vibes. Ferns and palms lined our route, and when I saw a donkey, I wondered if this was some sort of elaborate set up.

A house was sat sprightly on the side of the road with its identity painted in big red letters. This was 'Lot 217, 5 Mile'. Like a ten-year-old discovering that Santa Claus didn't exist and being the only one in your school class not to know (not that I'm scarred), it slowly dawned on me that Nine Mile is so named so because it is nine miles away from something. For fear of ridicule, I kept this realisation to myself. My guess is, that it is nine miles from the nearest big town, which is Claremont.

The stretch between Five Mile and Nine Mile is barren. It is very, very isolated, and not the sort of place you would like to be stranded at night. Pops was explaining that a school friend of his who had become a businessman had been robbed and murdered up here some years ago, one of a few similar incidents that was plaguing the area. The murderer was eventually tracked down and shot by Jamaica's finest and this area has been free of such episodes ever since. Suddenly, we turned a corner and an enormous dull-orange wall assaulted us. It looked like some kind of fortified base, and I immediately realised that this must be it. All those years of listening to the man, and here I was at his birth and resting place. Then a guy came up to the car and shouted "Hey, Bob Marley!" which appears to be the standard greeting aimed at anyone white in Jamaica. Remembering Mr. 'I am Bob Marley' in Claremont I gave him a wide berth as we entered the compound. The huge gates opened, and our vehicle was ushered in. Unfortunately, so was Mr. 'I am Bob Marley' Mk II. He asked if I smoked to which I replied in the negative whilst puffing furiously on a Craven 'A'. I knew what he was talking about, and he knew that I knew what he was talking about, but I was being clean today. He then offered to show us his plantation after our visit. I knew this would cost us so I told him I would think about it knowing that I still had about a quarter of the bag Pops had given me on Day 1 of my Jamaican odyssey. I was also just itching to get in to see the site upon which my young mind had been so inquisitive about all those years ago.

We paid our fee and moved upstairs, and having passed through some wonderfully ornate wooden frames we arrived at a set of wooden doors which were thick and heavy and bore a carving of Bob and a depiction of a lion on both sides. They looked incredible, but they were locked. We asked how to get in at Mama Marley's, the cash-in commercialist restaurant that is becoming something of a chain both here and abroad and were told we must wait for our guide. I instantly realised my worst nightmare was about to come true. I had avoided it thus far on the trip and so resigned myself to the fact that, for this once, I would be amongst a group of tourists. My fears were confirmed when a family of English brats stomped up the steps and proceeded to swarm and bounce all over the place causing absolute chaos. The kids stormed through Mama Marley's destroying all the carefully positioned menus on the table. Mom grabbed a menu and shouted to everyone who was unfortunate enough to be within range of her high-pitched shriek "Forget Bob Marley. This is what I have come for, the food!"

Her deserving of each other husband/fiancée/partner joined in and on seeing the restaurant shouted "Look at this! Bob lived it large, man!" seemingly oblivious to the fact that the restaurant, gift shop and fortified compound were not here when Bob was. You could tell that this lot were 'tick-list' travellers.

Dunn's River Falls? Been there? Tick.

Ocho Rios? Been there? Tick.

Montego Bay? Been there? Tick.

Bob Marley Mausoleum? Came, saw, and managed to ruin the visit for everyone else present? Tick.

I looked at Pops with a mixture of horror and self-pity. I was going to have to listen to this for the next hour when all I wanted to do was come and pay my respects to a man whose music had meant an awful lot to me. Pops gave me a glance of solemn recognition. He felt my pain. At least I was not alone. A group of Italians seemed equally appalled at having to spend any amount of time with the ADDAMS FAMILY from England. Our guide arrived and began to regale us with stories of Bob that were well known to most of us already. As a result, GOMEZ ADDAMS saw it as his job to attempt to preempt every word our guide was trying to get out. It was made more confusing because GOMEZ's 'facts' were blatantly incorrect. MORTICIA on the other hand was nodding sagely and taking everything in with a "Yeah, I know..." I was not going to let them spoil it for me, and so, short on weapons, I decided to slowly slope to the rear of the party. I was like a long-distance runner, appearing to go backwards as I was quickly overtaken

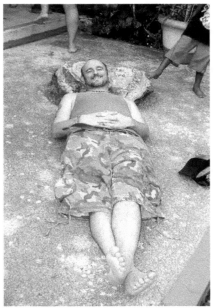

Isaac stoned

by the rest of the field. These English idiots must surely have known that this place, as well as being the site of his birth, is also the plot on which Bob Marley is buried and that as such, a certain degree of courtesy, decorum and respect is required, like in a cemetery for instance. Instead, they charged around like they were on speed in a supermarket sweep. I tried to ignore them the best I could and found it easier at the rear of the pack because they were busy trying to muscle in and take charge at the front.

The guide pointed to a corrugated roof below us, explaining that this was the house in which Bob was born. We then trooped through a courtyard where a Rasta was playing Bob tunes on a guitar. It appeared that this was all he did with his day; sit there strumming his instrument and singing songs in honour of the great man. What a great job! Some huge dark brown wooden gates barred our further entry. In the middle of them was a sign proclaiming that this was the Bob Marley Mausoleum. On either side was a picture of Bob, one topped with the word 'Respect' and the other with 'Exodus'. Before we could move further, I was distracted by the shrieks of children and scraping sounds down to my right where a huge iron gate stood. Suddenly, tiny little arms appeared underneath, hands cupped in fervent hope. It was the local kids begging for something, anything from our party. I was momentarily transfixed, but the rest of the group had already brazenly walked through the gates and up towards Mount Zion which is where Bob used to meditate. I vowed to see the kids on the way out.

The mound at the top which is also known as Sugar Hill is lined with flags from many different countries and the Union Flag of Great Britain was (despite the breeze) hanging her head in shame, probably at the behaviour of her embarrassing ADDAMS FAMILY ambassadors below. At the top of Mount Zion is where the history awaits. A mausoleum containing a huge marble slab has been erected and is the eternal resting place of Bob's mother Cedella, who died in April 2008, and to her right is the house that she and Bob moved into when he was six months old. It consists of only two rooms. The first is spartan, save for the posthumously framed photographs of Bob in action that hang from the walls. A beautifully carved bench sits there waiting for the return of its master. It is carved in the shape of a human and is a perfect fit for most of those gathered here who took turns at resting in it themselves, although for some of the bigger visitors there was some 'spillage'. Behind sits the bedroom, once more virtually devoid of decoration other than some badly pasted posters and a painting of Bob as a Christ-like figure. The bed is tiny and would need to be in such an enclosed space. This house attests to the fact that Bob was born into poverty. It has since been daubed with slogans such as *Love Jah Live*, which whilst a nice sentiment, rather takes away the feel of what it must really have been like when Bob lived here. In fact, the whole fortified nature of the compound with its expensive restaurant and gift shop has separated the Marley residence from the rest of the village, so it is difficult to fully comprehend how this tiny house would have fitted into the whole scheme of things within Nine Mile. Set back behind the house sits an immovable circular stone the size of a dustbin lid. It has been painted in the familiar Rasta colours and is apparently the stone that Bob described as his pillow in the song *Talkin' Blues*. The ADDAMS FAMILY kids were trampling all over it, as they had done all over Cedella Marley's Mausoleum. Just behind it stands another Rasta coloured construction which was the wood fire (stove) that Bob and his mother used to cook on. Rasta and Jamaican flags flutter wildly all around the compound and trees bear wooden plaques with *Rastafari* written on them. Everything has been painted in the red gold and green of Bob's Rasta faith, although our guide suggested Rastafari to be a way of life as opposed to a religion.

The final visit of the tour is to Bob's Mausoleum itself. It is a picturesque structure, church-like in demeanour and modest in size. The entrance is crowned with the words *Jah Love* and once inside photography is strictly forbidden. We all entered in a reverential and hushed awe befitting of being at the final resting place of such a legend. The actual slab of rock itself is massive, and unbeknownst to me it houses two bodies. Bob lies six-foot-high and facing the east whilst his brother Anthony, a victim of a police shooting in the United States, lies three feet below him. The magnificent rock was shipped over from Ethiopia, the Rastafari land of return. There was finally a respectful silence as our guide explained what some of the artefacts within the mausoleum were. I was simply stunned. Bob Marley's voice had always seemed to come from such a distant place; an untouchable and imponderable dreamland, somewhere I was never likely to go to or be able to comprehend. And here I was having achieved at least one of these aims standing next to the great man himself. Because of the timelessness of his music, it is still difficult to believe he is dead.

My reverential state of grace was interrupted by a sudden and enormous *Crrassssssshhhhhh!*

Everyone turned around in stunned shock. The sound had come from a narrow gap down the side of the Mausoleum. We all craned our necks around to where the deafening sound had come from, as the guide shouted at someone or something to come out. The eldest ADDAMS child sheepishly shuffled into view. This kid who thought he was street and had been sullenly walking around the site like someone who wanted to be anywhere but here had decided to shuffle down the side of Bob Marley's grave and dislodge something, the sound of which immediately prompted the thought "That's broken." The guide was positively enraged and saw fit to prematurely end our tour at this juncture and we sidled out, all cursing that awful family for not allowing our homage to last a little longer. We trooped back down to the restaurant and there they were again, the little arms scrambling underneath the iron door desperate for something to help them through their day. It was an incongruous site given that Bob was famous for his largesse. I tipped what money I had on me into their hands and moved on. One must wonder if, with their snazzy restaurants and lucrative merchandising spreading into Barbados and the United States and beyond, the Marleys' have lost touch with the message that Bob was trying to spread. I find it difficult to believe that if the Marleys' do still help the people of Nine Mile these kids were simply being greedy as there was too much desperation in their actions. I hope, of course, that I am wrong.

As if on cue, Jah then let his displeasure be known by sending down a veritable Biblical rainstorm onto the empty heads of the ADDAMSFAMILY as they scrambled down the steps towards their waiting bus. For the rest of us watching dryly from the gift shop, it was a blessing; both the rain and the disappearance of this embarrassing representation of England.

When it rains up in the hills it is something of wonder. At a suitable break in the conditions, we walked to the car, me pausing to look at Bob's birthplace one last time. Mr. "I am Bob Marley" Mk II had been washed away too so all was good and we could be on our way into the most delicious of scenes. Palms were bowing under a heavy wet weight with tears pouring down their faces, there was a strange but sweet smell of coal circling the ether, and everywhere clouds of steam glided between the trees and all was occurring in one of the most beautiful parts of Jamaica. After experiencing this scene, and if I get there, Heaven has a lot to live up to.

As we descended the nine miles towards Claremont, Pops was occasionally assailed by a roadside voice. I heard someone ask him if he was selling his car as we ambled by a group of church returnees, another simply shouted "Yo!" to which Pops responded with his car horn. We then saw the man with the doll again, determinedly carrying his 'child' back to from where he had come. Pops knew about the guy and explained that he was "crazy", and that every day he made the same two-way journey to go to one of the villages to smoke his weed before returning home. Crazy? Walking daily through this wonderful countryside; in these wonderful conditions, and all in a bid to numb himself to the troubles of the world? It sounds perfectly sane to me...except for the doll, perhaps. The Marley visit had been made something of a trial thanks to the ADDAMS FAMILY but at least I had done one of the things I came here to do; and had paid my respects to Robert Nesta Marley.

Chapter Twenty-Two

The Internal Struggle of A Superhero

I have caught the bug. Not another expression of my accompanying hypochondria, because this bug is vehicular. Having been without Gladys for a couple of days, I was feeling lovesick and desperately needed to see her again.

Unfortunately, she was no longer available (my suspicion is that she was on her way to the scrap yard) and so I was introduced to her upper-class sister. I decided to spice up my life and call her Victoria because this car was 'posh' in comparison to Gladys, who truth be told had long since waved goodbye to her best years. Even the brakes worked on Victoria. She was more of a family car, and I did not gain the same vicarious thrill as I had driving Gladys, but nevertheless she would get me from A to B so I committed my act of car adultery. I drove down to Ochi and visited the Scotia Bank to sort some money out. As I entered, I could not believe the absolute scrum of people inside. There must have been around a hundred customers, no doubt ensuring they had their dollars in hand to celebrate the forthcoming Independence Day on the 6th August. I have timed my trip well in being present on the island for three celebrations of real importance: Hailie Selassie's Earthstrong on the 23rd July, Emancipation Day on the 1st August and now the forthcoming Independence celebration. Once I had received my few dollars more, I went for a walk around Ocho Rios trying to avoid the continual hassles that I am prone to encounter due to my natural tourist-y appearance (even after a month I have defied the sun aside from my face and forearms) and the assumption therein that I am in need of taxis, trinkets or weed, which incidentally I have happily resumed consumption of in my bid to finish Pop's bag, well, it's not going to finish itself is it? When you smoke this stuff, everything you see and hear is turned up to full volume and in Jamaica that can only be a good thing. I gradually became aware of one persistent higgler who was marching behind me determined to get my attention. My patience finally snapped, and I swivelled round with a vicious look and blazing eyes, and he very quickly backed off. I had cracked it! All those hours of practicing a screw face as demonstrated by every one of my family at various points, often to ward off even the most forward of traders, had finally come to fruition. Previously I had looked as though I was either gurning, in pain or in need of the bathroom double quick. Not now. Now I feared no-one.

In Jamaica there are hundreds of thousands of people who really need help. At this point let me once more mention the tourist billions. Education is supposed to be free but really isn't, especially when you factor in the cost of uniforms, shoes, books, and food. The Health Service appears to be 'popped down'. Electricity is sporadic and non-existent in some of the darker recesses of the island, and from a purely selfish point of view, the roads are an absolute mess. The infrastructure of the country seems to need overhauling because the people, dem ah suffah. Unfortunately, as exists everywhere, there are unscrupulous types who are able bodied and who could be at least trying to do something instead of presenting a pastiche in the realm of the needy. Genuine desperation is impossible to miss. It is painted in the eyes.

Today I wanted to swim, but not in Ocho Rios' sterile and claustrophobic atmosphere. I wanted the fun, vitality, and effervescence of Jamaica, so instead I decided to put Victoria to the test and bolt down to Priory where I had swum in the early days of my visit. Once more it was wonderful, and once more I took on Lucifer's proportions in colour because today the sun decided to prove just how powerful she could be by sizzling me like a sausage. Even though I was being cooked, I spotted a cricket match unfolding and as I had with football on a previous visit to Priory, I asked if I could join in. I was a pretty good left arm over, fast bowler as a youth and had a trial with a County team in England so I knew I would be able to hold my own. My team were fielding first so I was directed to take up the unique position of, not slip, not mid-wicket not long-on but 'in the sea', I drifted off into a reverie recalling another childhood influence that was instrumental in building my admiration and love for Jamaica and the Caribbean generally. Growing up in Wales, there is a tongue in cheek tradition of wanting England to lose at any sporting event they might participate in. When I was growing up and when it came to cricket, the West Indies regularly hammered the English so they were my team. Of particular interest me was their four fearsome fast bowlers and in particular Michael Holding - Whispering Death - who was my favourite. He was named 'Whispering' because the umpires could not hear him approach and 'Death' because he was almost literally deadly. He is also Jamaican and since his cricketing career ended has become a much-respected commentator and even more recently a persuasive anti-racism spokesperson. I was moved to tears along with him when during the rise of the Black Lives Matter movement he recalled some of the strife his parents had been through at the hands of the scourge of racism. Back in 1984 the West Indies toured England and I was lucky enough to see them in action for two days at Old Trafford in Manchester. I was only young and on the first day I sat with my uncle in the general section but I was as mesmerised and transfixed by the exuberance of the West Indies fans as I was with the match, so on the second day I wandered off and sat in with the Caribbean crowd. They looked after me, shared food with me and there was a strangely sweet smell all around me that wasn't in the rest of the ground (my first contact hit), but best of all they were having a fantastically hilarious fun time watching their team wipe the floor with that symbol of Empire, the English cricket team. The game was dominated by Gordon Greenidge's double century but at one o'clock Michael Holding came over to chat with 'us' West Indies fans after he had helped move a sight screen (to a rendition of "Michael rowed the boat ashore, Alleluia").

Overwhelmed by it all, when I got home I sent my cherished programme off to the next venue and addressed to Clive Lloyd (my father's favourite player and the West Indes captain), *The Oval, Kennington, London SE11 5SS* with a polite letter included, asking if he might ask some of the players to sign it. A week after the final test finished, my self-addressed envelope arrived back at my house and so I nervously opened it hoping not to be disappointed. Not only was it signed, but every single player and the manager had signed the programme across their pictures. It is still my most treasured possession. This kind gesture, like Bob Marley's music, had a huge effect on how I viewed the people of Jamaica and the Caribbean and a long distance love affair with the place was further cemented, imbued with a great deal of admiration, respect, and affection. Following my reverie and having taken a catch and a couple of wickets on the sandy Priory pitch, I needed refreshment. I bought an ice cream from a man with a box on the back of his motorbike. I had watched him approach, and saw in my mind another Jamaican superhero, MOTORBIKE MAN, bringing fun and light into the hearts of young kids. As he got closer, I noticed that he seemed to be gaining an awful lot of pleasure in crushing the carefully crafted sandcastles on the shoreline to a cacophony of crying

Local dealer...in ice creams

and cawing. I wasn't bothered, I had a thirst. I yelled him over and he did one of those motor-cross spins, the type that sends sandy debris everywhere, in this case most of it thudding into the tiny faces of some children digging a moat. No bother to MOTORBIKE MAN. He simply straightened up and sent a high-speed smattering of sludge to coat their little backs as they ran to their mothers screaming. Oblivious to the bout of infanticide taking place in his wake he sidled up to take my order. MOTORBIKE MAN was one cool mother. He had a light blue baseball cap with *New York* emblazoned on it. He had a pair of swish Armani shading his stubbled face and he had a toothpick permanently lodged between his Clint Eastwood gritted grimace. He had on what looked like a blue and white nautical jumper, a pair of fresh Levi's, and some leather sandals. Like I said, he was one cool mother. MOTORBIKE MAN didn't say one word to me throughout the transaction, and he looked at me as though he was thinking deadly thoughts just before drawing at the O.K. Corral. He simply corresponded in gestures, one of which was a "So What?" shrug in the direction of the women and children hurling abuse at him. I think his name might have been *Bumbaclaat* because that is what I could hear the group of mothers yelling in the near distance. After much deliberation, I plumped for the enticing *Richie's Super Cone*. It should have been called *One Lick and a Cone* because that was all I got. It had melted by the time I raised it to my mouth for that second slurp. I turned round to utter a cheated "Hey!" but MOTORBIKE MAN was already off, laughing demonically as he chaotically swung and swerved across the beach, destroying further infantile architectural feats of wonder.

I philosophised on what I had just witnessed. In everyone there is the potential to do good or bad. MOTORBIKE MAN encapsulates the human split personality. On the one hand he is the vendor of *Richie's Super Cone* an ice to soothe the hottest of palettes (for at least five seconds anyway) and on the other a dark destroyer of the dreams of children. I hope that one day MOTORBIKE MAN will return as a real hero to those kids, teaching them the values of right and wrong, turning them away from all the evil in the world... sniffs.

Perhaps I simply caught him on an off day.

I climbed back into Victoria and we tore up to Pleasanton through what I now know is Steer Town, which is the village that possesses the cricket pitch in the heavens. On the way home I stopped off at Faith's Pen for some ital veg, festivals and bammies. I don't know exactly what a festival is, but I like it. With my renewed independence I thought, what the hell, I'll go for a drink. I stopped off in Claremont and walked into a bar. It was like a scene from a cowboy film. I swung through the doors (banged on the gate for someone to let me in), strode through the bar (tripped up the step), and ordered a whisky (said "Errrrr what have you got?"). There was only about six people in there, but I still felt like the last man in town given the claustrophobic space into which we were crammed.

Mr Wilson immediately began chatting to me.

He introduced himslef to me the minute I walked in and Mr. Wilson had travelled so we talked football teams and other related (to England) things. He plied me with drinks (including Rum Cream which I fully recommend) and then invited me to a party. Tomorrow was Independence Day, and Mr. Wilson was having a shindig at his place. He gave me some directions which I didn't fully understand, and then an itinerary of tomorrow's menu. It would begin with breakfast of 'run down' a local Jamaican food that is basically anything but cooked in coconut juice. I wanted a little more precision on the 'anything' but it wasn't forthcoming. Next up was Mannish Water (Goat Head Soup) followed by the rest of the unfortunate Nanny who was to be freshly slaughtered that morning. Mr. Wilson was a lovely guy. He was a bundle of laughs and had known me only ten minutes before he invited me to his party, and it was heartening to have such a warm gesture thrust at me through the night. However, I had other plans. I wanted to make one final journey to the house of someone who could only be a product of my own island at home. I had yet to see much of St. Mary where the subject of my quest had lived, so I decided that the coast road through the parish was worthy of exploration. I reflected on my newfound independence in Jamaica. My family had let me off my reins and I had survived and even prospered to some extent. However, I vowed that after the trip to St. Mary I would endeavour to stay with my family for the final day because I know what a sentimental fool I am, and I knew just how much I was going to miss them all when I had gone.

Chapter Twenty-Three

"Mad Dogs and Englishmen Go Out in the Midday Sun"

Today is Independence Day and the overwhelming vibe is laid back and lazy. Having experienced the virtual shut down on the island that was a feature of Emancipation Day, I realised I would have to make my own entertainment on this celebratory occasion.

If you are heading along the north-east coast having passed through Ocho Rios, you are in the Parish of St Mary. It is a lovely drive mainly because the roads are remarkably good. I passed through Bascobel, the first town of note which sits prettily on an ocean view. I then began to see signs for Oracabessa. I had heard of this place in relation to James Bond. Ian Fleming wrote several of his Bond stories here and some of the locations have been used in the movies. However, I was seeking literature of a higher brow and after an enforced detour through Oracabessa on a road that was the worst I have encountered yet, we hit a stretch of highway that was plain sailing and inches from the sea.

This is Chris Blackwell country. The Island Records impresario has always remained loyal to his Jamaican upbringing, and he lives in (and owns) a lot of this seemingly less tourist-driven Parish. There seemed to be an awful lot to discover but in my mind was one location, Firefly. I had heard of this village as a retreat of an actor, playwright, and composer who I fondly remember for his cameo in the original The Italian Job. I was shocked to hear such appalling language in such a fruity tongue from that ultimate English gentleman, Sir (lest we forget) Noel Coward. Yet amazingly, nobody I have spoken to here in Jamaica seemed to have heard of Firefly nor Noel

Coward, except for one. I stopped the car to speak to a Dread at the side of the road. His name was Lightning. I asked him if he knew where Firefly was. He affirmed that he did, and he told me a 'bredren' of his was the curator. He looked friendly enough and he told me he would take me up there. One thousand yards from where I had asked for directions, we took a sharp right on an unmarked road and began our steep climb. The drive was like passing through a miniature Fern Gully, driving higher and higher through the thickest of foliage. I was acutely aware that picking up a strange man by the side of the road and believing every word he said in a country that I am still trying to wrap my head around was not a particularly wise move, but I was becoming more confident in Jamaica, and I am a black belt in karate as well as several other more exotically named disciplines. Well, I went to a class once.

At this stage I had not decided whether to visit the museum or not because I thought I could just have a look around the town and then decide. Still, we climbed and then Lightning pointed me to the right and another forked road. We were being lifted towards the ceiling of Jamaica, and this was an enigmatic elevator ride. Finally, the yellow writing screeching from a blue background announced the fact that we had arrived. Firefly was not a town. It was simply Noel Coward's house and the grounds. The choice had been made for me. I had ended up here quite by accident really, expecting, if anything, just to pass through. Now I was going on a tour.

I hear you. Tourist!

I expected a similar nightmare to that at Nine Miles, bumping into fellow white people giving you a nod of recognition as if to say "Hey! Another white person!" and yet this was perhaps the quietest place I had been to on the entire island. It's Zen like demeanour was soothing after visiting towns and cities of

Isaac channelling his inner Noel Coward

sheer loudness and brightness. Walking through the front gates the first thing to be seen is a beautifully manicured garden that extends towards the horizon. Climbing through it, a flat white slab of stone is visible towards the top right-hand side of the garden. It is Noel Coward's resting place. It is perched upon the absolute edge of a cliff with a view of his own private paradise. When he departed to meet his maker, he must have hoped that it would be to this piece of land sitting on the edge of the world that he would be heading towards.

The Caribbean Sea swarms around a coastline of sunny wonder, and there in the middle, the mountains and the forest and the seas have come together to cradle a miraculous baby island. Huge languidly soaring birds roar their approval above. It is a breath-taking sight. To the left is Noel's blue and white and pristine house whilst just in the foreground is Noel himself. He sits in sculptured contemplation on exactly the spot he used to quite literally watch this magnificent world go by. The statue is a beautiful tribute to the man who loved the place so much that he wanted to stay here forever. He sits there, cigarette in hand, eyebrow arched and with that semi-permanent smile on his face; immaculately dressed of course.

Inside the house it seems like it has been practically untouched since Noel lived here. An open-air conservatory protects the same kitchenware that was laid out for the visit of the Queen Mother in 1965. After climbing the stairs, a rectangular room dazzles you in its natural wonder. Almost the whole of one side of the house has an enormous window cut into it with no glass enabling the astonishing view outside to be on permanent display. The vista is like having a huge painting spread across one wall. Lightning had been given carte blanche to show me around and he took full advantage of it, commandeering my camera and persuading me to sit in chairs, on beds and on balconies so that he could record my visit to this fantastic place. Everything seems to have retained its English/Jamaican charm even though Noel died as long ago as 1973. I was shown around his music room, his kitchen, his bedroom, and his lounge. Each had their own stamp of Noel Coward. Noel was a keen painter too and his studio still looks as though it is in use. Some of his paintings are very vibrant perfectly reflecting the Jamaica I have come to know. One representative piece was of some muscular young men stripping for the beach, reflecting Noel's other major interest. I can only imagine what Jamaica would have made of Noel Coward's homosexuality today, but I imagine that when he lived here, they were more innocent times, a time when homosexuality was not as much of an issue as it is today in the country.

I bought a drink from the bar in the grounds which apparently previously served as one of the real, genuine, bona-fide, lookout points of Captain Henry Morgan. I cannot imagine that there is a better one on the island. As a fellow Welshman I raised a toast to the pirate as I took in the picture postcard beauty. Firefly was a stunning surprise and so I spent the afternoon with Noel having drinks on the lawn.

By mid-afternoon my hunger for aesthetic beauty was sated but my real hunger was rearing its head, and so I said my farewells to Lightning and this little bit of England in Jamaica and headed back towards Ocho Rios. On the outskirts of Ochi is an area known as White River and the smell of cooked fish enticed me in. There was a river (that didn't look particularly white) running through it upon which various boats and tyres masquerading as people carriers, lazily drifted by. I went into the tiniest food shack I have seen thus far with room for approximately three people. Towards the back I could see reams of fish sitting in pots and pans, all appearing to be screaming for freedom such was the expression on their faces. I chose a yellow-coloured fish, and it was delicious. I have been told since it was a Parrot fish and despite my not being a massive fish lover, it was special.

As I ate I went for a wander, following a group of individuals lamb-like and heading through a field to the river. There they found a hole in the fence which allowed them to circumnavigate the official entrance to the gorgeous looking private beach. This required balancing on a ledge just wide enough for the tiniest of feet and clasping the wall whilst turning one hundred and eighty degrees before hitting terra firma once more. There were several huge splashes accompanied by lively laughter as some of the trespassers didn't quite manage to retain their balance. It was a holiday, and these people were making the most of it. I sat with my legs dangling in the river for a while and eating my fish before heading back to Pleasanton. I felt a little subdued because my time here was coming to an end. As I got closer to Ochi I chanced upon the most stunning woman I had ever seen in my life. It was her eyes that first entranced me, framed by a sculptured brow they positively dazzled from her fiery countenance. With full and sensuous pursed lips, cheekbones as sharp as razor wire and full and vibrant braids cascading down her shimmering shoulders and back, she was wading through the waters at Dunn's River Falls looking like perfection. She was about 12-foot-tall and adorned a poster advertising one of Jamaica's most famous beauty and tourist spots, the latter feature explaining why I had not bothered visiting. If the tourists weren't there and this girl was then I might have been tempted; but the former were certain to be there, and I was almost certain she wasn't.

The name Jamaica comes from the original inhabitants of the land, the Arawak. The Arawak were a mild mannered and peaceful people until they were all but wiped out by (not the English this time, their brutality would come later) the Spanish. "Xayamaca" means 'land of rivers and springs' and by all accounts Dunn's Rivers Falls is the most striking example of the Xayamaca, but it wasn't for me, not with lots of foreigners flopping and flailing over the place. I may have missed out on my dream woman but if it is deemed so by the magic of this land, she will 'soon come'.

Reminding myself that it was Independence Day, I hoped that Jamaica would be partying as only Jamaicans can tonight, just to cheer me up a little. Strangely though, the roads on the drive back were muted. Pleasanton was empty as were the towns of Moneague, Walkers Wood and Colegate.

This being my penultimate day, and therefore also my last day with a car, I considered the lack of crazies on the road a good opportunity to carry on driving through Moneague and heading over the border into St Catherine to search for that elusive vagina rock. I picked Buzzy up firstly for company, and secondly because he is the self-proclaimed expert in that field. We passed through Linstead and out the other side, and then on into the wonderfully named Bog Walk Gorge. The lack of traffic meant we could drive at a more leisurely pace. The familiar child salesmen and women were largely absent today, so any pining I had for guinep or mangoes would not be sated, but my desire to find the vagina rock would be.

"Look nuh Isaac!" demanded Buzzy pointing over to my right-hand side.

I turned my head and was blinded by an enormous and frightening looking vagina. How I had missed Pum-Pum rock previously (remembering the local patois name for this curiously aligned formation), I do not know. More polite circles refer to it as the nature rock yet there is no doubting it's resemblance to the particular anatomical structure after which it is named, and if it helps bring in a few tourists and a few 'dollars' for the local haggler kids, a 'slack' title might be forgiven on this occasion.

Mission accomplished, Buzzy and I headed back to Moneague. I had decided that an evening trip to Ochi might be required for me to see something of the Independence Day celebrations. And so, I put on my smartest clothes and went to ask the family for suggestions of where to go. Buzzy, who was still there holding court as evidenced by the raucous laughter, began to warn me away from certain places because they would be full of "white people". I did a double glance, and realising what he had said, and who he had said it to, he began laughing. He was not being insulting, because for him the term 'white people' in Jamaica is a synonym for tourists.

Driving in Jamaica at night is far more hazardous than driving in the day. For a start, you cannot see the edge of the road, the bends in the road, and in places, the road itself. Also, Jamaican drivers tend to drive with their full beam on regardless of whether there is oncoming traffic or not. This can mean that whilst trying to manoeuvre around certain hazardous hairpins you can also be blinded by the dazzling lights of oncoming vehicles. As for Fern Gully at night, I would hate to be trapped in there once the sun has dropped from view. The thick vegetation takes on a sinister bent especially considering that there are no lights anywhere through the 3km stretch.

Escaping out into the light of Ocho Rios was a relief. However, I knew I would be safe on this journey, because all the way I had been behind a Scooby Doo-like people carrier that had *The Lord is With You* and *Blessed Saviour* tattooed on its back. Occasionally, a fist thumped out of the window rhythmically, in time to the loud Gospel sounds pumping out of the van.

Ocho Rios tonight looked like Kingston on the evening I had been there. People swarmed the streets, drinking, shouting, and smoking. Buses roared aggressively through the highways and byways; horns were on permanent parp as they tried to warn the pedestrians that they would be stopping for no-one tonight. Leering glances and short skirts flirted with each other, whilst everyone seemed to be all over the roads and sidewalks.

I parked up and deciding to eschew Buzzy's advice, I headed for Margaritaville. I was leaving tomorrow and so thought I should at least try to discover what it was that my fellow non-Jamaicans did with their evening hours. Margaritaville is a nightclub. It is a busy nightclub, and it reminded me of when I was in my late teens in that it is basically a 'knocking shop'. It appears that men and women go there for one thing, and it was one thing that I was not interested in at this point in time. Having paid an entrance fee that guaranteed me free drinks for the evening, I had a Red Stripe but soon realised that this was what Buzzy had warned me about, and so soon left, trooping past the massive hordes of people waiting to go in.

I had decided that it would be far more entertaining to watch the locals become slowly and steadily more drunk in the streets and carparks of the town. After half an hour of people watching I decided to head back to Pleasanton and attempt to get a drink there before I went to my bed. Driving up through Fern Gully for the very last time, I decided to try to overtake the slow-moving vehicle in front of me. As I pulled level with my target, there was a huge CLUNK and my steering wheel fell away in my hands. I panicked, slammed on the brakes, and managed to tuck back in behind the car I had been trying to pass. The steering wheel had suddenly dropped down and was moving about alarmingly as I tried to negotiate the already difficult Gully. I had to drive the rest of the way with one hand under the steering wheel ensuring that it stayed at the correctheight whilst using the other hand to direct my movements.

Victoria had let me down. She was not 'posh' but simply a case of mutton dressed as lamb.

After arriving home and following the trauma of the drive, I went to my room and attacked a bottle of lethal Jamaican rum. I thought about the First World's approach to Jamaica; about the unseemly privileged and spoilt nature of a lot of the tourists I had just witnessed at Margaritaville, and conversely about the rampant poverty and the conditions in which the *sufferahs* must live.

The hands scraping beneath the metallic compound fences at Nine Mile will haunt me for a long time as will my concern for Jay's physical condition which by all accounts will worsen. I wondered if resort tourists ever get to see or consider the plight of many on the island. So, whilst I have focused on there being *Something to Smile About* in Jamaica, and there is so, so much, there is also plenty that needs addressing. My interview with the Minister of Tourism fell through in the end, but given the type of questions I wanted answers to it was probably best for both of us. Jamaica is a tourist paradise for visitors and a natural paradise for those who live here, but it is still a Third World country with a poor infrastructure and little sign that solutions will *soon come*. The people are fighters though and they will continue to make the best out of the situation.

My time here was coming to an end, and I knew I was going to miss everybody and everything about the country. A wave of melancholy hit me on the realisation that I would not be seeing these people and these places in twenty-four hours' time. I have never been particularly adept at goodbyes, and I really feared having to go through the process tomorrow in a Jamaica that I had fallen head over heels in love with.

Chapter Twenty-Four

"Mi Gaan"

The sun was glorious, the sounds melodious, and the smells gorgeous.

And I was leaving.

Aside from the enormous hangover I had engendered due to imbibing far too much Wray and Nephew the night before, everything was irie in Paradise.

And I was leaving.

Packing my cases was like the reverse process of when I first arrived. Once more a hive of industry swarmed my room and within what seemed like seconds, I was ready to go. Buzzy and Jay would be accompanying me to the airport, a journey I was looking forward to with the demeanour of a condemned man heading for the gallows.

The porch that had been the morning and evening meeting place for me and my wonderful family for the last month, was now subdued because it was the venue for my goodbyes. It seemed like every single character I had met over my time here had decided to drop in on me before I left. Keith ambled by and amiably expressed the conviction that I would be back. Michael arrived and stayed for a Red Stripe whilst I silently listened to the magnificent array of patois being shot back and forth, mostly concerning the forthcoming athletics meetings and the local hopes for Jamaican medals. Jonesy was back and his languid and relaxed aura made me temporarily forget that the next day I would be back in the hustle and bustle of old grey England.

Then Buzzy arrived.

At this point, Pops rolled me an enormous farewell joint and I began to say my goodbyes. Poochie, Snoop and TJ gave hugs and kisses. DeeDee, Jay, Kadee and Kaydee followed suit and I was given a Rasta necklace and pipe from Ras Kelvin in his absence. I bumped fists with Radar before exchanging massive hugs with Pops and Momma. Every single one of these beautiful people had in some way, small and large, made me feel that leaving them was akin to experiencing bereavement. I had experienced a majestic month here, and every character present had contributed to the fun, enabling me to feel welcome and secure in an entirely different but wonderful and mysterious culture.

And I was leaving.

Being stoned did not help matters, as it only accentuated the feeling of loss that I was struggling to cope with. As I waved my goodbyes, I was close to tears, and I am sure I glimpsed a few in the eyes of my family too. I had a steady supply of weed and booze to ease me on my way to Montego Bay but it wasn't enough. We moved out of Plesanton heading for a destination I did not want to arrive at. As we by-passed Ocho Rios, Jay's phone rang. It was Ras Kelvin. During my trip I had been asking about the possibility of getting some Lignum Vitae seeds, Jamaica's national flower, to take home as a natural souvenir and a piece of the land. However, I had been told that it was the wrong season and despite my visiting a number of garden centres on the island, I had little success in tracking down this seemingly elusive symbol of Jamaica.

Kelvin's call was to suggest we drop in on him on the way to the airport as he had managed to get some seeds for me. And so Buzzy took a left off the main road and we headed up a beaten track and parked next to some sturdy trees. When we got out of the car, Ras Kelvin was nowhere to be seen but I could hear the repetitive thud of metal on wood from behind the trees. As we ventured around to where the noise was coming from, the kind of surprising site that I had now come to expect in Jamaica appeared like a vision before me. In a shaded covering of brightly coloured and perfumed trees was a cluster of Dreads all busy shaping magnificent artefacts from enormous chunks of wood. In amongst them was Kelvin.

On seeing me he sprang to his feet, and with a big smile on his face presented me with half a tree with a beautiful purple flower attached. After much debate we decided that I would not be able to take this tree halfway across the globe, so we detached the seeds from their safe haven within the flowers and I placed them in my wallet for safe keeping. I should have guessed that one of these amazing and lovable people would come up trumps!

After this beacon of altruism, I could only brood further on the fact that I was leaving it all behind. At the airport, further handshakes with Jay and Buzzy were administered (Buzzy's variant being extremely convoluted, and I still had not got the hang of it even after a month) and then I was on my own. I watched forlornly as Jay and Buzzy returned to their car without me. Faced with the terrifying prospect of flight once more, I did what comes naturally; I hit the bar. By the time my flight was called I felt suitably and drunkenly prepared for the ensuing journey.

I checked in my bags, before being interrogated by a drugs officer (returning from Jamaica with the surname *Hye* I guess it was more than likely that I would be checked out - but at least there was not a rubber glove in sight), and then as I was close to boarding, I was approached by airport staff as there appeared to be a problem. I was not going to be allowed on the plane with the beautifully carved stick that Ras Kelvin had gifted me. I had christened it my 'rod of correction' since a similar moniker was given to former P.M. Michael Manley's stick that he had received from H.I.M. Emperor Hailie Selassie, and I was panicked by the thought that our separation might be made permanent. It was suggested that I get it wrapped, and in fact on entering the airport someone had offered to do this, but in my now Western focused and sceptical mind I had imagined never seeing either the 'wrapper' or the stick again. I felt happier that one of the airport staff would be monitoring the process now, but would not be entirely happy until me and my rod were reconnected on British soil.

My seat was once more positioned behind a gargantuan man who made FATFOOTBALLHEAD look positively dwarfish. This man was wearing a shirt the size of circus marquee and when he squeezed himself into his seat you could hear it cracking and creaking in pain. He was virtually on my lap for the whole journey.

I had been 'on the go' for nearly five weeks solid and so consequently once I had eaten my 'food' I soon dropped off, probably because of the booze/weed combo that was still fuelling through my veins. In fact, I woke only once more to eat before dropping off again and in seemingly no time at all I was awoken to strap in for the landing.

London was cloudy and as the plane dipped through the grey bubbles of sludge streaking the sky, it was making all sorts of random movements, but after my five weeks of spiritual nourishment I was comfortable in the knowledge that Jah would protect me. When we landed, the iron bird positively bounced off the tarmac about three times as the customary applause kicked in.

The scramble for bags ensued and I stopped to check with a flight attendant that my rod of correction would be waiting for me on the carousel. I was told it would be, and yet after waiting for an hour or so I had my bags but still no stick. I then saw a passenger with golf clubs and asked if he had been allowed them on the plane. He explained that he hadn't and that he had picked them up from a separate area which he then directed me to. When I arrived there, my rod sat forlornly on his own. I picked it up and I must have looked like a Zulu warrior riding my trolley through customs, especially so when I punched my rod in the air as I passed golf club guy.

Once outside the terminal I sparked up a cigarette, but then realising that my throat was dry I decided to pop back in to buy a drink from the vending machine. By the time the coins had popped through the slot, I had encountered a volley of abuse from various passers-by for smoking inside the terminal. My reaction was simply to glare and shrug my shoulders, a tip picked up from MOTORBIKE MAN.

My car was waiting for me, in one piece but with a slight flat more than likely a result of my fight with a kerb on the way into Gatwick all those weeks ago. I didn't think I was fit to drive but I nevertheless steeled myself for the hour and a half journey. It was six in the morning, but it felt like the middle of the night. Suddenly, whilst still on the M25 I heard an enormous clunk followed by the sound of what I can only describe as a continuous scrape. My exhaust was hanging off. My car was no Gladys.

Having finally stuttered home, thrown my bags down, turned on the television and made myself a cup of tea, I began to reflect on my Jamaican odyssey. As if by magic, the first thing I saw was Jamaica's athletes strolling onto my screen, no doubt preparing to make the world sit up and take notice of this wonderful country once more. I closed my eyes and drifted off.

I dreamt of myself perched on the edge of one of the cliffs at Firefly but instead of the stunning sight that one can normally see from that vantage point, I was being afforded a view of the whole island. Montego Bay was there; sparkling and shining to the thunderous night-time beats of Sumfest. Ocho Rios was teeming with tourists, hagglers and higglers. St Elizabeth, where rural beauty soothes her people through the hard times, and St Thomas bathed in natural jaw-dropping splendour were jammed with Jamaicans smiling and joking through their tough lives. There sat Kingston, vibrant by day and unpredictable by night. And then I saw them; slap bang in the middle of the island stood the beautiful people of Pleasanton my home from home. I leant over the cliff edge and squinted hard and I could see my house and my family all looking into the sky at me, waving towards me, and wearing the biggest warm and beatific smiles. I zoomed out again and could see the whole of Jamaica as if from space. As I looked to my left, I saw the spirits of Nanny and Marcus and Paul watching over the island whilst to my right, Bob's Natural Mystic was flowing through the air. I could see it, sloping to the rhythm of those who walk the land, ensuring that the spirit that makes Jamaica such a special place remains for eternity.

Interviews

Jamaican's Jamaica

I interviewed several musicians at Sumfest and one of the questions I asked them all was what Jamaica meant to them. It seems only right therefore that last word should be left to some of those charged with promoting the island to the world via their mesmeric music.

Stacious (female singer)

"For me, Jamaica is me. It is in everything I do, and I gain great pride in representing my country. The Jamaican people are colourful and artists such as Bounty Killer, Lady Saw, Queen Ifrica, Ken Boothe, Bob Marley are the artists I see myself following. I think Bounty made a mistake this weekend, but he will recover".

Pressure (Rasta, and conscious artist)

"I see Sumfest as keeping reggae alive and exposing artist's talent. It is love through music. Jamaica has done a lot for me in my life, and I want to give something back, especially regarding the poverty here. Rastafari can help the world. Love - the world needs it. The Jamaican people have always supported me, and Jamaica is reggae, a music spreading black awareness".

Anthony Able (Rasta and conscious artist)

"Sumfest means expression. Anthony Able to the world! Rastafari is my life, and it means I love my friends and neighbours. Rasta is Mother Nature, and we should love each person on this earth with no colour but one family. The Jamaican people need help especially with regards to education. Brutality is a result of a lack of education. In Jamaica Rastafari is not respected, yet it is around the globe. The government needs to help the people and turn us away from sadness."

Prophecy (Rasta and conscious artist)

"Rastafari needs to spread the message of love and peace. Events like this can only help. We need more Marcus Garvey and more Bob Marley. Jamaica is an island full of lovely people, here is where it's at! I am a son of this island and I represent my country and reggae music. Reggae can help give the island an economic boost which will in turn help my people".

Lutan Fyah (Rasta and conscious artist)

"Sumfest is a celebration of music, and it is the biggest three nights of the year. It is a privilege to perform here, and it gives Jamaica positive vibes. I and I is a Rasta, and His Imperial Majesty and Africa are my passions. The Teachings of His Imperial Majesty give us a grasp of knowledge of man. The Jamaican people are a loving people, they look on the brighter side of life. Jamaica is my homeland, I was born here, but my passion is Africa which I see as uplifting to the black race".

Queen Ifrica (Rasta artist straddling both conscious and dancehall genres).

"Jamaica is where mi come from and Sumfest helps promote the island. My Rasta beliefs are centred around equal rights and fighting the black and white downpressers. Things can be changed by individual people, but we need to stay positive and change ourselves. The Jamaican people are burden bearers, but they carry the burden with a sense of fun, with music and dance allowing them some relief from their struggles. Jamaica is a little dot on the face of the earth, but it is responsible for music you can hear on any street corner around the globe. Jamaica is strong when united, but that unity has been exploited. We need to acknowledge where we are in the world and live together in peace!"

Jah Cure (Reggae artist and songwriter).

"Sumfest and Jamaica come together in their love for music. My Rasta faith has been passed down through my grandmother, my father, and my mother. The Jamaican people are so loving but on the other hand they can be violent, but Rastafari stresses the positive of life, love, and music. What does Jamaica mean to me personally? Jah Cure!"

Etana (Rasta singer and positive female role model for the young people of Jamaica).

"This is my second Sumfest but this year has been much better. Marcia Griffiths is my inspiration since she explained certain things as a woman that you can carry with you through life. The Jamaican people, wow, they are so loving and sharing but they can have their faults such as greed and envy, but there is much more love in them especially amongst the garrison people. 'Nuff Love but greed, envy and poverty are the problems. Rasta is a good example in life because women have a voice. The creation suggests that women came after animals, but the Empress never walked behind a man. Jamaica to me is a number of things, but it's in my roots, in the hills, in the congo drums and in the elders' stories that bring us closer to our ancestors".

Isaac Hye (author, weed smoker, general buffoon).

Jamaica to me is all of the above, but in my time there, it was most certainly a land of love.